THE SHAPE
OF THE DANCE

Also by Michael Donaghy

Dances Learned Last Night:
Poems 1975–1995

Conjure

Safest

Collected Poems

MICHAEL DONAGHY

THE SHAPE
OF THE DANCE

Essays, Interviews and Digressions

Edited by Adam O'Riordan and Maddy Paxman

PICADOR

First published 2009 by Picador
an imprint of Pan Macmillan Ltd
Pan Macmillan, 20 New Wharf Road, London N1 9RR
Basingstoke and Oxford
Associated companies throughout the world
www.panmacmillan.com

ISBN 978-0-330-45628-9

1 3 5 7 9 8 6 4 2

A CIP catalogue record for this book is available from
the British Library.

Printed in the UK by CPI Mackays, Chatham ME5 8TD

Contents

Introduction

The Donaghy Negotiation

Michael Donaghy's death at fifty was a cruel blow but he had already done enough as a writer of poetry to establish himself firmly among recent poets who matter. His achievement as a writer about poetry, however, is still in the process of being assessed and absorbed. The first and best thing to say about his critical writing, I think, is that it was necessary, even when that fact was not yet generally realized. If we can see now why his views on poetry were so vital, it is because they help us to recognize what was missing. Nobody else in his generation had such a generous yet discriminating scope. It is still the kind of scope we need, but now we have his example. He called true poetry 'the alchemical payoff', and his criticism shows how prose can be that too.

Born only two years before Allen Ginsberg's *Howl* was published in 1956, Donaghy grew up as an Irish Catholic in New York at a time when American poetry was supposedly breaking its last bonds with the transatlantic formal tradition. He was never automatically contemptuous of the results that accrued to this final freedom. He just doubted its validity as an historical movement. Whether by instinct or from his training as a musician – questions of underlying psychology preoccupied him all his short life – he was suspicious of the idea that freedom from all restriction could yield perfect creative liberty. (He often insisted that even *Howl* was not the Whitmanesque 'barbaric yawp' that Ginsberg claimed, but a carefully worked and reworked artefact.) At Chicago University, where Donaghy edited the *Chicago Review* and founded his music ensemble, he was already grappling with the critical questions that arose from a too confident assertion of American separateness.

In pursuit of his future wife, and perhaps also in pursuit of a more nuanced context in which to work, he moved to London in 1985, and steadily established himself as an imported expert who knew more than the locals. Actually this, too, was an American tradition that went back as far as Henry James, T. S. Eliot and Ezra Pound, not to mention the Eighth Air Force during Word War Two, but his presence was refreshingly new to a whole generation of young British poets who came to his classes. The impact of his own collections of poetry might have been enough to pull them in, but his powers as a mentor kept them glued to their chairs. There was a paradox in that. Donaghy never ceased to warn against the menace of the 'creative writing' industry on either side of the Atlantic: hundreds of creative-writing teachers with nothing useful to say, thousands of creative-writing students publishing first collections that would go nowhere.

But his British students knew that they had found a teacher who transcended his own suspicions. At least a dozen gifted young poets benefited from his combination of a wide-ranging sympathy and a tight focus on language. If they are now a school without a name, it was because he taught them the merits of unbelonging. He had an even wider field of influence, however, through the pieces he wrote for such outlets as *Poetry Review*. Many of these pieces, undertaken as journeywork at the time but always lavished with the wealth of his knowledge and the best of his judgement, are collected in this book, and it is remarkable how they coalesce into the most articulate possible expression of a unified critical vision. He was a crucially important reviewer, and my chief concern here is to say why.

When reviewing another poet, Donaghy relied first and foremost on his ear for loose language. Devoid, on paper at least, of malice or professional jealousy, he could nevertheless quote a dud line with piercing effect. Robert Bly thought he was being profound when he wrote: 'There's a restless gloom in my mind.' Donaghy could tell that whatever was happening to Bly's mind at that moment, it wasn't profundity. But he made such judgements a starting point, not a death sentence. What had the same poet written that was better? Donaghy could quote that, too. He was always searching for the language that had reached a satisfactory compression and power of suggestion. (It didn't have to come from 'the tradition', or even from a poem: he was a close listener to song lyrics, playground rhymes, and street slang.) When he found it in a poem, he had his principles to help him explain it.

To his chief principle he gave the name 'negotiation'. A sufficiently tense diction, the alchemical pay-off, was, Donaghy argued, most likely to be obtained from a contest between what the poet aimed to say and the form in which he had chosen to say it. If the poet tied the creative process down to his initial commitment, with no formal pressure to force him to the unexpected, there was no contest; and a contest there had to be, no matter how loose the form. Always a great quoter, Donaghy, on this point, quoted Proust to telling effect: 'The tyranny of rhyme forces the poet to the discovery of his finest lines.' The tyranny didn't always have to be of rhyme, but there had to be some tyranny somewhere. Negotiation was Donaghy's touchstone concept, and lack of negotiation was the reason why he thought an informal poem was even more likely to slide into banality than a formal one. When he found intensity within an apparently formless work, it was because the author had imposed some kind of discipline upon himself, locally if not in general. He found a good example in C. K. Williams, whose ten-beat loose lines had, in Donaghy's opinion, an underlying formal drive, proving that something concrete had been negotiated even when the poem steered towards abstraction. This capacity to find practical merit even in what he was theoretically against was a precious virtue.

It was matched by an equal capacity to find the limitations even in what he was theoretically for. John Updike's poetry was as formally virtuosic as might be wished, but Donaghy thought that too much of it was too much so. There were too many poems that 'almost made it before the skill took over'. The implication was that a display of skill should not be an end in itself, even though to eschew skill altogether was a bad way of avoiding the danger.

In this way, Donaghy left a door open so that he get back to the informal spontaneity of American modernism after William Carlos

Williams and praise it where praise was due. His openness to the possible strength of the informal poem lent him the authority to say that the rewards from a formal poem could be greater, just as long as they had been properly negotiated. But he was certain that the informal poem had far more dangerous ways of going rotten than the formal one. When the formal tradition decayed, the result was, at worst, sclerosis: a malady whose chief symptom he neatly summed up as 'rhyming in your sleep'. But the informal tradition in decay was an infinitely adaptable virus which would always try to pass itself off as the next development of the avant garde. Donaghy the mighty quoter liked to revisit his favourite quotations, and the one that he revisited most often was from Auden. 'Everything changes but the avant garde'. But the witticism isn't the whole truth. The avant garde does change, in its scope: it continually increases its territorial claims. Logically it should have run out of steam when the ne plus ultra stood revealed as the reductio ad absurdum some time during the reign of Dada, but here we are, almost a hundred years later, and there are still poems exploding all over a full page in the *London Review of Books* like fine shrapnel, just as if Apollinaire had never done anything similar.

Donaghy, not very neatly for once, referred to such abjectly posturing stuff as L=A=N=G=U=A=G=E poetry. He was borrowing the title of the busy movement's home-base magazine, but he might have done better just to call it poppycock. Large-heartedly, he found enough time for this tirelessly self-propagating fad in which to decide that it added up to nothing. (His rejections were seldom immediate, but they were always decisive when they came.) Donaghy's British acolytes were not encouraged to follow the example of those established poets, often well protected within the academy, whose poetry is beyond criticism because it is about nothing except language. Donaghy wanted his young hopefuls to write negotiated poems, which are never just about language even when they say they are. Some of his modern models were British, or at any rate Irish: he said he didn't mind being asked to talk about 'Auden & Co.' as long as it was understood that the 'Co.' meant MacNeice. There was a whole teaching programme hidden in that one remark, because it will always be true that a neophyte stands to learn more from MacNeice than from Auden: it is useful, if frustrating, to try copying MacNeice's strictness, but it is fatal to try copying Auden's apparent nonchalance.

But for his British students and readers, Donaghy's most provocative models for the accomplished poem were Americans. His range of examples drew from the two great lines of achievement leading on from Whitman and Emily Dickinson but he lent no credence to schools, only to the intensity of the individual talent. In one of his reviews, he ascribed to Richard Wilbur 'the most flawless command of musical phrase of any American poet.' It's a mark of the consistent authority of Donaghy's critical prose that the confidence of such a judgement sounds precise, instead of just like a puff on a jacket. In the quarter of a century before Donaghy became active as a reviewer, the outstanding critical voice in London had been Ian Hamilton. Nobody wrote a better argument than Hamilton, but not even once did he say something like that about Wilbur, or indeed about anybody. Hamilton was strongest when he found weakness. Donaghy, in so many ways the heir to Hamilton's seals of office, was no more forgiving to lax expression, but far less inhibited about communicating enjoyment, instead of just leaving it to be inferred.

Donaghy was not immediately famous as a critic in Britain, whose citadels fall slowly. But he was immediately understood: the broad sympathy of his view travelled well. Especially he was understood by his young admirers, to whom he gave, by his guidance of their reading, the modern American poetry that matters. Indeed he gave them America, with the result that some of the best poems about America in recent years were composed in Britain by young writers who had got their standards for highly charged and musically cadenced language from him. We all enjoy such a coup as Frank O'Hara's poem about Lana Turner, and even those of us who think that John Ashbery has turned into a factory get a kick out of his classic poem about Daffy Duck. But not even O'Hara or Ashbery ever wrote anything quite as good about American popular culture as John Stammers' poem 'The Other Dozier'. Once it would have been a sign of cultural subjection for Britain to claim that some of the best American poetry is written here. Now it sounds more like a simple claim to truth: the Atlantic has become an exchange of energy, and Donaghy is partly responsible.

He was also responsible, and more than partly, for ensuring that some of the best American criticism would be written here. He might have found it harder to write it at home, where any critic who publishes a limiting judgement is thought to be an assassin. In a previous generation, the same had been thought of Randall Jarrell, but in fact Jarrell could be adventurous and generous in his praise: nobody, not even Galway Kinnell when introducing his indispensable selection from Whitman, could do a better job than Jarrell of showing why the best lines and phrases from *Leaves of Grass* defy belittlement even at their most naive. Jarrell's strength as an appreciator, however, depended on his powers of discrimination, and that dependency will always be regarded with suspicion in America, where a critic sins against democracy if he finds some poets more valuable than others. Donaghy, who had already committed the same offence, probably did well to head for less tolerant climes. And after all, he brought the best American criticism with him, just as he brought the best American poetry. Donaghy regularly paid his fellow American critics the tribute, with due acknowledgement, of reproducing their best lines. Thus we came to hear Dana Gioia's opinion that ideas in the poetry of Ashbery are 'like the melodies in some jazz improvisation where the musicians have left out the original tune to avoid paying royalties.' Donaghy knew he couldn't beat that, so he quoted it. But there were many occasions on which he matched it. He could deliver judgements in a way that people remembered, and for anyone who is capable of doing that, it really matters if he is right or wrong.

In his theoretical work it mattered less. Quite a lot of Donaghy's writing on psychology is included here. The general reflections on creativity that arise from these studies are invariably valuable, but in the end there is no settling some of the conundrums about the functioning of the brain: or anyway, if they ever are settled, it probably won't be by a poet. Perhaps partly because of the traditional

Introduction

nostalgia of the lapsed PhD, science always fascinated him. He not only admired Coleridge, he emulated him, producing pages of text in which various parts of the argument go on in various frames, rather as *The Rime of the Ancient Mariner* grew annotations in the margin. But such pretensions to complex simultaneity weren't what made Coleridge a genius, they were what ensured his genius would never be coherent. Donaghy was in no such danger, because he knew what came first: the sayable, memorable, living poem, and his living response to it. Science didn't even come second. His repudiated but never forgotten Catholicism would have a better claim to the silver medal. When he talks about poetic truth, he just can't help mentioning the Elevation of the Host. Ritual was deeply embedded in him, like music. They were formal resources. But every resource of his mind and memory was in service to language, of which, both creatively and critically, he was a master. Had he lived, he would surely have done such great things that he would have been universally recognized as one of the voices of his time, not only in poetry but in the understanding of it. Some of the reasons we can be so sure are in this book.

CLIVE JAMES
London 2008

WALLFLOWERS

*A lecture on poetry with misplaced notes
and additional heckling*

Cuius rei demonstrationem mirabilem sane detexi hanc marginis exiguitas non caparet. *

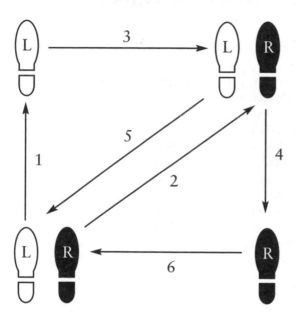

* I have a truly marvellous demonstration of this proposition which this margin is too narrow to contain.

– Fermat

1 Telling the Dancer from the Dance

Reader in
Residence:
Your attention,
please. This is
not a digression.
This is your
representative
jotting a note
in the margin
on your behalf.
Imagine for a
moment that you
are not merely
reading this note,
but thinking in
these very words
as you read them
and our task will
be much easier.
We think
Mr Donaghy is
about to be
extravagant,
anecdotal, and
self-dramatizing.

ALL MY LIFE I have harboured a weakness for those wilfully eccentric philosophical and theological precepts valuable for their beauty alone, like Swedenborg's fancy that, in their purity and selflessness, angels create space instead of taking it up, thereby dilating the pin upon which they dance, or the North African Gnostic idea that all material beings are 3D letters in the penmanship of God, or the Cabalistic fear that when, in the next great age, the Hebrew letter *shin* grows a fourth vertical stroke, a new sound will utter from men's mouths, making pronounceable the hitherto unpronounceable name of God – at which precise moment the world will end.

Having thus disqualified myself from the role of earnest philosopher, I'd like to share with you my own homely addition to this aviary of ideas, a minor epiphany concerning the relationship of the poet and the reader . . . This idea occurred to me one rainy night about twenty years ago in a church hall on the south side of Chicago.

. . . I'd been playing jigs and reels for a ceilidh, watching the set dancers spinning and stamping out with wild precision the rhythms of a dance which can be described (accurately) as a feral minuet. Some time during the course of the evening the music I had for years only heard and played became visible, filled with spinning sweaty couples, as the abstract shape of a whirlpool fills with water, or an equation takes shape as a tetrahedron. Only after the dancers had left the floor did I notice the circular patterns of black scuffs and streaks their heels had made on the polished wood.

This pattern, I recognized, was an enormous encoded page of poetry, a kind of manuscript, or, more properly, a *pediscript*.

If I were standing before you saying this, you wouldn't have to read it. These lines are instructions for your voice to mimic mine (you may not be moving your lips as you read, but your breath and throat muscles are changing subtly in response). Just as a

My uncle Jack Sheehy, traditional musician, the Bronx, 1955.

manuscript is a set of rules for summoning the speaker (from beyond the grave, if necessary), the pediscript is a set of rules for executing the dance.

In order to interpret that dance chart you've got to get up and move (imagine describing a spiral staircase with your hands behind your back, or a chess game without a board and pieces). But your dance partner is long gone. All that remains is a diagram, or the black streaks on the floorboards.

Like all literary poetry in our culture, the pediscript is the record of – or formula for – a social transaction, all that remains of that give and take between artist and participating audience in an oral tradition.

It's not my intention here to underrate or dismiss the enormous intellectual advantage in being a wallflower at that dance. But the wordless dialogue of dancers and musicians in the dance hall, the dancers' relationships with one another . . . Over that next year or so, I began to compare that order of experience, *bodily* experience, with my academic experience of poetry.

This was 1977. Then as now, the term 'tradition' was politically charged for academics and intellectuals. For them it suggested orthodoxy, exclusivity, and their own disputed canon of prescribed masterpieces of European culture. But I grew up among several communities of immigrants in New York City – Italian, Irish, Puerto Rican – who regarded their oral traditions as a covenant with their respective cultures. A player in such a tradition is expected to improvise, to 'make it new', and the possibilities for expression within the prescribed forms are infinite. But it's considered absurd to violate the conventions of the form, the 'shape' of the dance tune or story, because you leave the community of your audience behind, and you bring the dancers to a standstill. By 'traditional form' I mean the shape of the dance, those verbal and rhythmical schemes shared by the living community which link it to the dead and to generations to come.[1] I'm not making a distinction between

---

1. Before writing existed, the only way to transmit important information from one generation to the next was to cast it in a memorizable form, to make it a song, for example, or a ritual dance, and this is still the case in cultures that have no written language. Systems for memorizing data are called mnemonics after Mnemosyne, the muse of memory, and these systems provide a clue to the origins of poetry. Rhyme, for example, is one such technique. How many days are in April? Before answering, most people instinctively run through the rhyme 'Thirty days have September, April, June and November . . .' Spell 'receive': '"i" before "e" except after "c"'. Another common technique is to associate units of information with words in a sentence. What are the notes on the musical scale? Most novice musicians remember that 'Every Good Boy Deserves Favour'. Yet another way involves the use of imagery; paired items, an angel and a crown, say, can be learned more rapidly if they're associated in a simple sentence – the angel is given the crown. The best way is to make pairs of items interact in some way – the angel dons the crown – and then link those items with a third, the crowned angel unfurls a scroll, and keep the chain going. In mnemonics, stories are often spun out of the need to remember the images they contain – in literature it's often the other way round.

The 'forms' to which I refer here are shapes, like the 'schemes' of classical rhetoric – *parachesis*, *hypophora*, etc – the artificial patterning of words, as opposed to 'tropes' like imagery. We must distinguish between memorability and memorizability. A rhyme or rhythm makes a point memorizable; a slap across the face (like a 'striking' image) makes anything memorable. In the absence of working schemes, artists have to slap a lot of face to have any noticeable effect.[1a]

1a. The footnote is my voice, of course, but in a slightly hushed tone, to distinguish it from the body of my argument.

'form' as that word applies to, say, iambic pentameter and the form of a twelve-bar blues, or a Petrarchan sonnet and a playground skipping rhyme.

If we were discussing this in person, I'd roll up the carpet and illustrate my point by marking out a diagram on the floor. But first let's consider just what a diagram is. It's a schematic picture, certainly, like a graph, a map, or a geometric proof, and we all accept nowadays that pictures are highly conventional, no matter how naturalistic they may appear at first glance. It's said that Picasso was once challenged by a model's husband who complained that the picture he'd painted bore little resemblance to his wife. 'What does she look like?' asked Picasso. The man took a snapshot from his wallet. Picasso squinted and said, 'She's very small, isn't she?' And, of course, he might have added that she was two-dimensional, monochrome, motionless, cut off at the waist, and that only the tip of her nose was truly in focus. Like the model's husband, we're tempted to accept pictorial conventions as natural, and our senses of scale and perspective, even our sense of beauty, are often modified by the conventions of image-making.

Maps and blueprints are pictures too. They function as instruments to help us to construct buildings or find our way through a city or forest by omitting most of the detail in order to emphasize the relation of a few relevant parts. And sometimes the conventions are relatively easy to spot. We know, for example, that a map is usually an aerial view with north at the top of the map and west to the left. We all know that when we look at a map on a wall we don't go north by flying straight up to the ceiling. The map of the London Underground is very useful in getting from A to B, but Londoners know it's worse than useless for getting

about on the surface. And certainly no one expects a house to resemble a blueprint. Geometrical proofs are a special case. These are the only diagrams that don't distort because they operate on the level of the ideal, purged of the noise of the real world. So geometry is pure diagram: the scheme or shape of a triangle or square or circle defined by a 'key' or 'legend' of equations using arbitrary markers – what mathematicians call 'variables'.[2]

But when the diagram represents a process unfolding in *time*, the hazards of oversimplification in any picture are even more insidious because the conventions of the picture can't be checked against the visible, tangible, apparently stable world. When, for example, we see a diagram depicting species 'developing' in branches from the root of a schematic tree, we're slipped a specious subliminal message beneath this visual metaphor, that living species are 'higher' than extinct species and somehow superior to them when in fact evolution is a response to arbitrary environmental changes ('the survival of the fittest' may be better expressed as 'the survival of the survivors'). This dubious message, that the rudimentary past is somehow perfected into the present, underpinned the Victorian notion of 'progress' and figures in a lot of twentieth-century ideas about art and literature.

Or consider the illusions built into that animated diagram of time itself, the clock face. Every day we experience both the usefulness of clocks and watches and their utter inadequacy in representing our real experience of duration. That last hour in bed with your

---

2. Michael Serres has a beautiful and fantastic hypothesis about the origin of geometry: Democritus and Plato both say the Greeks crossed the sea to educate themselves in Egypt. The problem, of course, is that the Egyptians wrote in the ideograms of hieroglyphics and the Greeks used an alphabet, a system of arbitrary signs to represent sounds. Geometry, he says, originated in the blending of those two systems of writing into a game in which they are utterly interdependent and describe nothing but each other. The square, triangle, and circle, he says, are all that remains in Greece of hieroglyphics.

lover and the next hour waiting for the
night bus in the rain are only the same to
your watch. Whenever we speak of 'Time',
that abstract generalization covering the
infinite variety of change taking place all
around us, we speak in simple spatial
metaphors; we say, for example, that it
'moves forward' and it was until recently
commonly expressed that some cultures
were 'backward'. Even our self-perception
is informed by the diagram; models of the

mind from Associationism to Freud and Jung depend on
visualizable diagrams of mental processes. Even in our
ordinary use of words like introspection we locate
consciousness inside our heads. We imagine a roomy
mental arena, which we usually locate inside our brains,
though other cultures have placed it in the heart or the
guts. But a close look at our terms reveals this as just
another spatial illusion. You can 'see where this is lead-
ing'. I'm 'approaching' a 'deep' problem, one I've kept
at 'the back of my mind'.

In non-literate cultures, of course, the only way to
preserve knowledge is to make it memorizable,[3] and the
most efficient way to do this is to render that knowledge
into a mental pattern – an invisible dance which only
comes alive with the participation of an audience. This
even holds true for classical oratory. From antiquity to

---

3. Aboriginal Australians believe that their ancestors sang the world into existence
during their walkabout in the Dream Time and that the world's existence can only be
maintained by keeping faith with tradition – going walkabout and navigating by singing
the 'songlines' (footnotes like this are a matter of creative juxtaposition. Gilbert Watts,
in his English version of *De Augmentis Scientarum* (1640), inveighed against the other
sort of footnote or marginal note, the citation of authorities:

> . . . *as if the Truth they deliver were to be tried by voices; or having lost its primi-
> tive innocence, must be covered with these fig leaves; or as if the Authors
> themselves were afraid that it should make an escape out of the text, were it not
> beset in the Margin with Authorities as with a watch.*

Wallflowers again).

the Renaissance, the rhetorical art of memory entailed the committing to memory of real or imaginary buildings such as temples, law courts, or cathedrals. A speaker could commit to memory, for example, the four virtues, the seven deadly sins, or a list of Roman emperors, by associating each in succession with the fixed parts of the building. To facilitate this feat of memorization, each part of the building would be equipped with a highly symbolic figure or striking image, to help fix the point for both the speaker and the audience. The individual alcoves or columns were known as the rooms or places, and this comes down to us today in expressions like 'topics' of conversation (from *topoi*, place); a 'commonplace' meaning a cliché; or in the *stanza* – Italian, room – of a poem.[4] *Strophe*, another kind of stanza, described a dance in the Greek choral ode, the chorus pacing in one direction chanting the strophe and back again chanting the antistrophe, arranging the parts of the song in theatrical space.

With this in mind – and the front of your mind will serve as well as the back – consider how any printed page of verse or prose, with all its paraphernalia of paragraphs, running heads, marginalia, pagination, footnotes, titles, line breaks and stanzas, can be understood as a diagram of a mental process.[5] And consider how much more insidious or convincing those conventions are when

---

4. Donne alludes to this kind of poetic space in 'The Canonisation':

> *We can die by it, if not live by love,*
> *And if unfit for tombs and hearse*
> *Our legend be, it will be fit for verse;*
> *And if no piece of Chronicle we prove,*
> *We'll build in sonnets pretty rooms;*
> *As well a well-wrought urn becomes*
> *The greatest ashes, as half-acre tombs,*
> *And by these hymns, all shall approve*
> *Us Canonised for Love.*

5. And sure enough, our word diagram derives from διαγραμμα, which doesn't distinguish between a geometrical figure fixing the relation of parts from a written list.

the diagram itself is invisible – I mean this as no airy metaphor: the words in the centre of the page surrounded by their somewhat reserved audience of footnotes and marginalia are a diagram of self-consciousness, a commentary frozen out of the flow of the story, song, or poem, out of the voice we've entered as we participate. In the extremest sense, the sense of the oral tradition, of the centre of gravity of all poetry, the sense of children's bedtime stories and ritual dramas like *Oedipus Rex* or the Mass, the audience are participants in total immersion, surrendering consciousness and voice to the story. But to read critically, as poetry readers do, alone in bed, or at their desks, or huddled together around the workshop table – wallflowers – is to scribble in the margin. The page encourages an illusion and seduces us with its model of the mind.

First digression

In 1798 Wordsworth and Coleridge, weary of some of the literary conventions of their day, invoked a different, perhaps more mannered set of oral conventions in their *Lyrical Ballads*. Coleridge's opening contribution to the volume was 'The Rime of the Ancyent Marinere' – to all appearances an hallucinatory, ergot-fuelled sixteenth-century ballad drawn from Gothic Romance, *The Arabian Nights*, and Renaissance travel books. There's a Latin epigraph from Burnet, an 'Argument', and then we're right into the thick of the tale.

> It is an ancyent Marinere,
> And he stoppeth one of three:
> 'By thy long grey beard and thy glittering eye
> 'Now wherefore stoppest me?

'The Bridegroom's doors are open'd wide
'And I am next of kin;
'The Guests are met, the Feast is set, –
'May'st hear the merry din.'

This is, in other words, the story of the story. The wedding guest could well be the reader's representative or listener in residence.

But still he holds the wedding-guest –
There was a Ship, quoth he –
'Nay, if thou'st got a laughsome tale,
'Marinere! come with me.'
He holds him with his skinny hand,
Quoth he, there was a Ship –
'Now get thee hence, thou grey-beard Loon!
'Or my Staff shall make thee skip.'
He holds him with his glittering eye –
The wedding-guest stood still
And listens like a three year's child;
The Marinere hath his will.
The wedding-guest sate on a stone,
He cannot chuse but hear:
And thus spake on that ancyent man,
The bright-eyed Marinere.

Seventeen years later Coleridge presented a new version in *Sybylline Leaves*. Alongside the outermost margins of the open book there now appeared a marginal commentary, a pastiche of a seventeenth-century gloss, like evidence from which the reader deduces the presence of an imaginary scholar explicating the imaginary poet of a story of a story being told.

An Ancient	It is an ancyent Marinere,
Mariner meeteth	And he stoppeth one of three:
three Gallants	'By thy long grey beard and thy glittering eye
bidden to a	'Now wherefore stoppest me?

wedding feast,	'The Bridegroom's doors are open'd wide
and detaineth	'And I am next of kin;
one.	'The Guests are met, the Feast is set, –
	'May'st hear the merry din.'

It was Coleridge who introduced the term *marginalia* to English from Latin. Some Coleridge scholar ought to consider the way Coleridge used peripheries – introductions, margins, and footnotes. From the introductory anecdote to 'Kubla Khan' to the grand hypertext of his *Biographia Literaria*, Coleridge exploited the physical space of the printed book to point up its illusions and suggest the living presence behind the words.

A brilliant stroke! Coleridge has interposed another reader between us and the text, and found a use for all that blank space in the left-hand margin.

End of digression

Duly cautioned as to the treachery of diagrams, let's move on to my own. Let this blackboard represent the dance floor. Just as musicians play for dancers, poets write for readers (or listeners), so let these two be our leading couple.

Mr Donaghy is gently moving us into position. Is this where we're supposed to stand?

For the poet (upper left), form functions as a kind of 'frame' or 'scaffold' from which the poem can be constructed. Stravinsky maintained that only in art could one be freed by the imposition of more rules, perhaps because these rules limit the field of possibilities and escort us beyond the selection of tools and media to laying the first stone of the work itself (of course, once the basic structure is built, rooms, *stanzas*, can be altered from the inside).

For the reader (upper right), the shared language of the poem functions as a com-

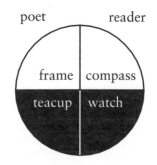

pass or map to assist us through the terrain of a new idea. Traditionally, narratives or arguments are parsed into, for example, episodes in which three wishes are granted, or rhetorical points explored. Physical expressions like 'On the one hand . . .' warn the listener to bracket the ensuing information and prepare for its antithesis '. . . and on the other . . .' These phrases exploit the reader's or audience's expectations, which, on a larger scale, is the aspect of tradition routinely targeted by the avant garde in this passing century as vulgar, bourgeois, and tranquillizing.[6]

Are we being insulted?

So much for the conscious operation of these schemes. Now let's look below the surface, to something I find far more mysterious, the unconscious or subliminal effects of reading and writing in traditional form. The unconscious effect of form on the reader I identify by the icon of the watch.[7]

We are hypnotized or spellbound by form because the traditional aural techniques of verse, the mnemonics of rhyme, metre, and rhetorical schemes, are designed

Attention. We are considering the effect of this image: Mr Donaghy is holding up a watch. It resembles the hypnotist's dangling fob watch familiar from end-of-the-pier shows and B-movies ("Your eyes are getting heavy").

6. Another aspect of audience expectation is the display of *conspicuous, publicly perceptible effort* and mastery of form – tacit agreements in the great unwritten contract between artist and audience. In Renaissance Italy the master painter, sculptor, dancer, musician, or poet was an *Amatore delle difficulta* – lover of difficulties. Lorenzo de Medici, for example praised the form of the sonnet 'arguing from its difficulty – since noble accomplishment (*virtù*), according to the philosophers, consists in the difficult'. Nor is the familiar popular reaction to modern painting and poetry – 'my five-year-old can draw better' and 'it doesn't rhyme' – the exclusive reserve of philistines who value over Picasso, say, scale models of cathedrals made from matchsticks. Modernist critics and literary historians also regard laborious and time-consuming composition as evidence of artistic integrity.

7.   *Beyond the name there lies what has no name;*
       Today I have felt its shadow stir the aim
       Of this blue needle, light and keen, whose sweep
       Homes to the utmost of the sea its love,
       Suggestive of a watch in dreams, or of
       Some bird, perhaps, who shifts a bit in sleep.

From 'The Compass', Borges, trans Wilbur.

to fix the poem in the memory, to burn it in deeper than prose. And because it stays in the memory a split-second longer, because it '*sounds* right', it seems to *be* right. Advertising copywriters and political speech writers know this, and take advantage of those venerable schemes of classical rhetoric to convince us below the level of reason, to sell us fags or governments.

Take *chiasmus*, for example: at John F. Kennedy's inauguration Robert Frost was scheduled to read his poem 'The Gift Outright' which began with the lines 'The land was ours before we were the land's . . . Possessing what we still were unpossessed by, / Possessed by what we now no more possessed'. Shortly afterwards, Kennedy's own speech contained the calculatedly memorable line 'Ask not what your country can do for you. Ask what you can do for your country.' The content of Kennedy's sentence is political propaganda, Frost's 'a momentary stay against confusion', but both share the familiar shape of 'Beauty is truth, truth beauty' like a dance step in which two couples change partners – never mind that beauty and truth can only be identical from a viewpoint shared by God, Grecian urns, and mathematicians. Or consider the appealing symmetry of 'An eye for an eye and a tooth for a tooth' – hardly a useful sentiment in the late twentieth century, but the rhetorical shape seems to validate and mask as an allegorical figure of Justitia our base instinct for revenge.

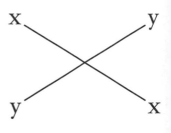

These formulae are the verbal equivalent of the pictorial space of the diagram and, as such, they are equally insidious. Les Murray has said that rhyme functions with the symmetry of logic. The terrifying truth is that form *substitutes* for logic. This is the poet's unique power, to address the passions in their own language, the very power that got us barred from the Republic.

Finally, let's consider the unconscious effect of form on the poet. This is the most interesting aspect of traditional technique, and it represents the intervention of that presence poets used to call 'The Muse'. Any degree of difficulty in a form requires of the poet that he or she negotiate with the medium, and compromise what he or she originally 'spontaneously' intended to say (so far so good, since one's instantaneous reaction is always more likely to be full of self-deception, prejudice, and cliché).[8] Perhaps many of us here have experienced the peculiar sensation that the best image or line simply 'came to us' as if delivered by an unseen presence as a reward for taking the time to work hard on a poem. It comes from our own unconscious, of course. The feeling of 'otherness' is explained by the fact that our self-perception is firmly rooted in our waking consciousness.[9]

I represent this aspect of form with, of all things, a teacup. I'm alluding here to the late American poet James Merrill who, like Yeats, claimed to have contacted

---

8. Leonardo criticized the painters, who, as he put it, 'want even the slightest trace of charcoal to remain valid', and asked them: 'Have you never thought about how poets compose their verse? They never trouble to trace beautiful letters nor do they mind crossing out several lines to improve them'. He wanted to warn artists to keep their compositions 'provisional' until they hit upon a radiant form, and warns against a method which would tie their creative process down to the original commitment. He advises the painters that they should 'be ready to change course at any moment, like the poet'. I for one have never ascertained how long I have to think of something before it stops being spontaneous. Perhaps it's not a matter of duration. Perhaps true spontaneity takes its own time.

9. See 'The Feeling of a Presence and Verbal Meaningfulness in Context of Temporal Lobe Function: Factor Analytic Verification of the Muses?' Persinger, Michael A.; Makarec, Katherine, *Brain and Cognition*, 1992, November, Vol 20 (2): 217–26. Persinger and Makarec hypothesize that the profound sensation of a presence, particularly during periods of profound verbal creativity in reading or writing prose or poetry, is an endemic cognitive phenomenon. Factor analyses of twelve clusters of phenomenological experiences from 348 men and 520 women (aged 18–65 years), who enrolled in undergraduate psychology courses over a ten-year period, supported the hypothesis. The authors conclude that periods of intense meaningfulness (a likely correlate of enhanced burst-firing in the left hippocampal-amygdaloid complex and temporal lobe) allow access to nonverbal representations that are the right hemispheric equivalents of the sense of self: they are perceived as a presence [from the Abstract].

and drawn on the assistance of 'the other side'. In the opening scene of his supernatural epic *The Changing Light At Sandover*, Merrill and his partner are playing about with a Ouija board. Suddenly, the upturned teacup they've been using for a pointer is commandeered by the soul of one of Caligula's murdered slaves. The spirit, Ephraim, answers their questions instantly, and largely in rhyme and metre. Later, Merrill refers to the attraction of the 'bedevilling couplet' and it's clear to this reader, at least, that Merrill's supernatural familiars are in part metaphors for the shaping forces of verse technique. John Ashbery has used a more mechanical metaphor to describe this effect. 'The really bizarre requirements of a sestina', he told *New York Quarterly*, 'I use as a probing tool rather than as a form in the traditional sense . . . rather like riding downhill on a bicycle and having the pedals push your feet. I wanted my feet pushed into places they wouldn't normally have taken'. But surely this is *precisely* the function of 'form in the traditional sense' that serendipity provided by negotiation with a resistant medium.

I began by warning against the dangers of simplification inherent in all diagrams, so I ought to dismantle my own. Any act of communication begins with imagining oneself in the place of potential readers or listeners in order to anticipate one's effect. Agreed? It could be said, then, that the poet *equals* the reader, because poets are themselves readers in the tradition of poetry, because poetry is in itself a way of reading in that tradition, and because poets are the first (and sometimes, sadly, the only) readers and critics of what they've written. Conversely, reading is a form of ventriloquism: sensitive readers give themselves up to the poet for the duration of the poem. (The night I watched those dancers in Chicago I realized the same relationship obtained in other traditional arts. When a *shannachie*, or traditional

I really must object on the reader's behalf. We've spent valuable time and energy visualizing Mr Donaghy's diagram and now he sees fit to erase it.

storyteller, spins his long tales, the reaction of the listening audience is part of the event, just as the reaction of the dancers complements and completes the music. As Borges says in his essay on Shaw, the poem is properly a dialogue with the reader and the peculiar accent he gives to its voice, the changing and durable images it leaves in his memory. That dialogue, he says, is infinite.)

So my diagram is really a kind of equation, and the condition of all equations is the resolution to equality of terms on either side of the equal sign.[10] It follows then that the frame or scaffolding of form is really no different from the compass and map of our own expectations as readers. And the spell induced by the hypnotist's fob watch, that power of subliminal persuasion, is the same spell the Muse exerts over our own imaginations.

Certainly poetry can address our rational side, but just as it gets its power from a place beyond reason, it affords us the power to address, represent, or exploit that same dangerous territory. Surely, one of our duties as twenty-first-century readers and poets will be to explore the political, however personal or oblique our approach, and that exploration will require questioning, dubiety, speculation, analysis. But as poets we have that unique power to address the passions in their own language. Perhaps our challenge, as we gradually leave the age of print, will be to discharge our writerly, civic duties from this platform without bringing to a standstill those rapt, whirling dancers just visible beyond the glare of the stagelights – amongst whom we might just glimpse ourselves.

---

10. 'Pronouns in poetry are like the "x" in algebra. Much of the enjoyment of reading certain poems involves the "solving" of the poem/equation's values for "I" and "U"' – Thom Disch.

2 Reading in rhythm

NOT LONG AGO I found myself engaged in a curious and ambitious translation project with a number of deaf poets who composed in sign language. By way of introduction to their craft they showed me a photocopy of a poem by the American deaf poet Clayton Valli. I was acutely embarrassed by the apparent mediocrity of the work and when I asked my signing interpreter to rescue me from this diplomatic disaster, she suggested we watch a video of Valli performing the poem in American Sign Language (ASL). It was extraordinarily beautiful and a clear example of Frost's dictum 'poetry is what's lost in translation', for this performance was the poem. The photocopied sheet on my lap was no more a work of literary art than a choreographer's stage directions can be said to constitute a ballet, or a pediscript a pavane.

'How can we tell the dancer from the dance?' Yeats asks in 'Among School Children', to which the uncowed reader may respond 'Why try?'. And here it seemed equally pointless to separate the poem from the bodily presence of the poet. The signed poem rides on the carrier wave of the signing poet's bodily rhythm and uses regular repetition of glance, nod, handshape, headshake, and innumerable other subtle physical signals the way audible verse

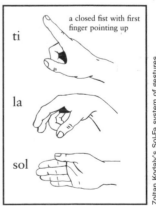

ti

la

sol

a closed fist with first finger pointing up

Zoltan Kodaly's Sol-Fa system of gestures for tone production

uses rhymes or refrains. 'Silence' is a slight pause, or a long freeze at the conclusion of a context. Signed poetry establishes its artificiality, its departure from conversational signing, by conscious grace; often the poet breaks eye contact, slows down, and divides signing between both hands for visual balance – broadly speaking, by returning language to dance.

The historian R. G. Collingwood, who called dance 'the mother of language', recognized that all language is rooted in the fact of bodily presence.

> We get still farther away from the fundamental facts about speech when we think of it as something that can be written and read, forgetting that writing, in our clumsy notations, can represent only a small part of the spoken sound, where pitch and stress, where tempo and rhythm, are almost entirely ignored . . . The written or printed book is only a series of hints, as elliptical as the neumes of Byzantine music.

Neumes?

Why, 'neumes' are those little strokes indicating pitch and vocal ornament accompanying the chants in ancient missals. Neumes were the predecessors of modern musical notes, originally Greek textual accents that were gradually modified into shapes so the monks could freeze the plainchant out of time, store it, and sing it back to life . . . chironomically.

Pardon?

Do keep up. Chironomy is the art of gesticulation or mime.[11] The monks would trace the sacred words in the

---

11. 'The original meaning of cheironomy as an art of bodily gesticulation, not confined to hands and arms as suggested by the Greek name, should be considered. The latter term was itself probably coined by taking the most striking part for the whole. It is not surprising, therefore, to find that in the Jewish tradition the head and the back as well as the hands are employed in spatial writing. Their respective functions are clearly defined. Of the three, the hand is the proper didactic medium for elementary teaching in religious schools (cheder) . . . Here is the place of the didactic hand 'waving' and 'winking' (neuma) used by the teacher to indicate the general outlines of the melody, and – even more so – its continuous flow and its animated spirituality (pneuma)'.

from the *New Grove Dictionary of Musical Instruments*, Macmillan, 1984, quoted in Ciaran Carson, *Last Night's Fun, A Book About Irish Traditional Music*, Cape, 1996.

air as they sang, hands wafting incense, deploying pitch and rhythm in space. Let's extend the word 'neumes' here to name those gestures.

There are few things that divide poets more than the concept of rhythm, and deaf poets are no exception. Clayton Valli even encountered a number of excessively politically correct (hearing) students in one of his workshops who objected that his lecture on rhythm was 'inappropriate'. But surely rhythm is far too complex and wide-ranging a phenomenon to limit to its auditory aspect. There's a convincing argument that poetic rhythm precedes both our visual *and* auditory fields, that it's innate, hard-wired into our brains: *The Neural Lyre*, a bizarre and wonderful collaborative study by poet Frederick Turner and scientist Ernst Pöppel, claims nothing less than a vindication of regular poetic metre in terms of brain physiology. Inspired by recent discoveries in human cortical information-processing that the left hemisphere of the brain maps spatial information onto a temporal order while the right hemisphere maps temporal information onto a spatial order, they argue that metre is in part a way of introducing right-brain processes into the left-brain activity of understanding language. Furthermore, they say, the brain possesses an auditory information 'buffer' of three seconds' worth of information (There! Now you know how long the present is!) and that this corresponds to a culturally universal and fundamental unit of metered poetry they call a LINE. In all the world's poetry, from Japanese to Ndembu (Zambia) to English, this unit falls within a 2.20 to 3 second cognitive cycle.

Obviously, this essay appeals to me on the level of strangeness and beauty. Since antiquity, poets and critics have sought to describe verse in terms of the living body – the 'organic analogy' and its related values of coherence, integration, synthesis, and closure.

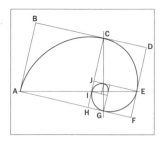

Take the celebrated number sequence discovered by Leonardo Fibonacci of Pisa in 1202 – starting at 1, each subsequent number is the sum of the two preceding numbers (1, 2, 3, 5, 8, 13, 21, etc . . .). Dividing each number in the series by the one which precedes it produces a ratio stabilizing around 1.618034, also known as the Golden Mean, the ideal proportion beloved of classical and Renaissance painters and architects, and which occurs as a logarithmic spiral in countless natural forms such as the conch shell, the arrangement of leaf stems on the stalks of plants, and the spiral distribution of seeds in the heads of sunflowers. The American poet John Frederick Nims has argued that this same ratio conforms to the original proportions of the Petrarchan sonnet. (Question: Is the sonnet built on the Renaissance sense of classical proportion or did it evolve naturally, out of the innate ordering principles of our minds?)[12] Even the most tedious and unmusical poets and critics of the twentieth century have sought to justify their sense of form by organic analogy: that the line corresponds to breath, or iambic metre to the heartbeat. Paul Lake argues that conventional forms like sonnets and villanelles 'evolve, like plants, through a process of iteration and feedback. The regular meter of formal poems is not a dull mechanical ticking, like a clock's; it coalesces out of the

---

12. The trouble with this neat theory is that the sonnet would need to stop at 13 lines to fit the Golden Mean. Scottish poet Don Paterson provides an ingenious way of saving this play by moving the goalposts: 'Let me run this one by you: one and thirteen are the same number. We often use the number twelve to indicate a cycle, so that the 13th instance of something brings us back to the position of the first, one cycle further on; think, for example, of the hours on the clock, the months in the year, the notes in the scale. The thirteen-line sonnet is symbolic of both transformation and unity – we've returned to precisely the same point as we started but have ascended in pitch or moved forward in time: so in the song's singing, in the idea's thinking, it's transformed, but stays the same' (Don Paterson, *101 Sonnets: From Shakespeare to Heaney*, Faber, 1999).

rhythms of randomly jotted phrases through a process of "phase-locking" – a natural process that occurs . . . when many individual oscillators shift from a state of collective chaos to beating together or resonating in harmony . . . the way the randomly flickering lights of fireflies become synchronous throughout a whole tree, and the way the menstrual cycles of women living in close proximity often phase-lock into a single, collective rhythm'. (From Paul Lake's 'The Shape of Poetry' on Arthur Mortenson's website *Expansive Poetry and Music Online*.)

Cough. Let us draw a curtain across this line of enquiry and move on.

3 In and out of the frame

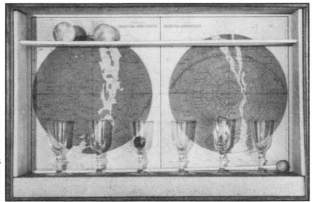

 Joseph Cornell, *Guiditta Past (Dedicace)*, 1950. Tate Gallery, London 1999.

CONSIDER NOW the work of the American artist Joseph Cornell: a self-taught slightly mad introvert from New York, he worked in surreal miniature dioramas, arranging his materials – trinkets from Woolworths, children's handbooks of astronomy and birds, thimbles and seashells and broken crystals – into intimate, mysterious shadow boxes. Perhaps because of the way he synthesized his materials within the enclosure of the box so that it became a little theatre or *stanza*, critics have often called his work 'poetic'.

Academics use the word 'closure' to mean the strategies poets use to give their poems a sense of conclusion – the big build-up at the end, the clinching rhyme. I use the term '*en*closure' to describe the way in which a poem is established as All-One-Thing. In Joyce's *A Portrait of the Artist As A Young Man*, Stephen Dedalus, out for a walk with his friend Lynch, points to a basket a butcher's boy is carrying and uses it to propound a theory of art based on a phrase from Aquinas: *Ad pulcritudinem tria requiruntur; integritas, consonantia, claritas* ('Three things are necessary for beauty; wholeness, harmony, and radiance').

Karol Kozlowski

integritas

Enclosure in poetry is the first step to what Joyce calls 'radiance'. Poets often play with the boundaries of the poem, exploiting an irresistible human instinct: just as we stare ink blots in a Rorschach test into the shapes of clouds or people or animals, we long to wrest coherence and integration from the structure of a poem. And as readers we're willing to go more than halfway to accommodate the poet.

A further word on frames: by an accident of typography the printed poem is traditionally laid out as a block of text in the centre of the page. This frame reinforces the impression that every poem aspires to a rectilinear condition, the shape of a mirror or a window. Windows show us the world outside our rooms, but when night falls and we switch on the lights we see only ourselves reflected in the dark glass, and sometimes, briefly, we mistake our own image for a presence outside. Mirrors, on the other hand, show us ourselves, but years on when the silver backing wears away we see past ourselves to whatever lies beyond.

So it is with poems: in our unconscious desire to locate the presence of the poet behind the frame of the words, we try to animate the poem itself (the organic analogy, see section II, above) and the poem itself seems to be *returning* our attention, or we attempt to breathe life into the inanimate.

Borges shows us a knife:

> A dagger rests in a drawer.
> It was forged in Toledo at the end of the last
>   century. Luis Melián Lafinur gave it to
>   my father, who brought it from Uruguay.
>   Evaristo Carriego once held it in his hand.
> Whoever lays eyes on it has to pick up the dagger
>   and toy with it, as if he had always been on
>   the lookout for it. The hand is quick to grip
>   the waiting hilt, and the powerful obeying
>   blade slides in and out of the sheath with
>   a click.
> This is not what the dagger wants.
> It is more than a structure of metal; men conceived
>   it and shaped it with a single end in mind.
>   It is, in some eternal way, the dagger that last
>   night knifed a man in Tacuarembó and the

daggers that rained on Caesar. It wants to
kill, it wants to shed sudden blood.
In a drawer of my writing table, among draft pages
and old letters, the dagger dreams over and
over its simple tiger's dream. On wielding
it the hand comes alive because the metal
comes alive, sensing itself, each time
handled, in touch with the killer for whom
it was forged.
At times I am sorry for it. Such power and single-
mindedness, so impassive or innocent its
pride, and the years slip by, unheeding.

('The Dagger', trans. Norman Thomas Di Giovanni)

And here's another knife, wielded this time by Eliza-
beth Bishop (speaking in the guise of Robinson Crusoe
in her dramatic monologue 'Crusoe in England'. This is
an excerpt from the end of the poem):

Now I live here, another island,
that doesn't seem like one, but who decides?
My blood was full of them; my brain
bred islands. But that archipelago
has petered out. I'm old.
I'm bored too, drinking my real tea,
surrounded by uninteresting lumber.
The knife there on the shelf –
it reeked of meaning, like a crucifix.
It lived. How many years did I
beg it implore it, not to break?
I knew each nick and scratch by heart,
the bluish blade, the broken tip,
the lines of wood grain on the handle . . .
Now it won't look at me at all.
The living soul has dribbled away.
My eyes rest on it and pass on.

'It reeked of meaning, like a crucifix', 'It lived', but now 'it won't look at me at all'. Consider those two notes: the numinous and the animate (it looks or does not look at you). One can't help but remember here the closing lines of Rilke's great poem 'Archaic Torso of Apollo': 'For here there is no place that doesn't see you. / You must change your life.'

Now there's a common species of lyric poem which takes as its organizing principle a single dominant object called, depending on which corridor of literary history you're exploring, an image, emblem, or conceit. With the reader's permission, I'd like to introduce the term *talisman* to describe the objects we've been discussing, because it carries a suggestion of that original, pre-literate animist mentality where poetry, mnemonics, and magic are mixed together.

I haven't yet forgiven you for 'neumes'.

Exactly. The *neume* is the gesture or flourish with which the poet produces the *talisman*. There's a species of modern poem that can trace its ancestry to the still life in painting – W.C. Williams' famous red wheelbarrow of 1923, for example.

So much depends . . .

Look, do you mind? I know it's your brief, but these interruptions are playing havoc with the flawless architecture of my argument.

Just trying to help.

This species of poem arose, I think, in reaction to the romantic lyric in which the poet's emotions were the subject of the poem. Of course, in Williams' poem, they still are. 'So much depends' upon this ordinary object but for whom does it depend? The emotionally charged inanimate object is a commonplace of twentieth-century verse in English, indicative, perhaps, of a retreat from abstract nouns like *honour* and *valour* in the wake of the Great War. As Williams himself cautioned, 'No ideas but in things'.

Modern poets often build their poems about a single point of emotional focus analogous to a point of optical focus in photographs – often represented by a single object held, like Yorick's skull, in the poet's hand, a magician's prop toward which we direct our attention so that the magic can proceed by sleight of hand.[13]

---

13. In psychoanalytic terms this object has an infantile precedent in what D. W. Winnicott calls the 'transitional object'. Most infants have a bit of old rag, blanket, particular doll or teddy bear which they cherish for months or years. Winnicott argues that these objects help us mediate, in developmental terms, between the experience of self and non-self. It's our first metaphor, invested with the power of the breast. Furthermore, says Winnicott, the mental space it occupies for us is neither subjective nor objective but 'there is the third part of the life of a human being, a part that we cannot ignore, an intermediate *area* [my italics] of experiencing, to which inner reality and external life both contribute. It is an area which is not challenged, because no claim is made on its behalf except that it shall exist as a resting place for the individual engaged in the perpetual human task of keeping inner and outer reality separate yet inter-related' (1950, p230). For Winnicott, all art begins in the transitional phenomena of infancy, the zone between subjectivity and objectivity (see D. W. Winnicott, *Playing and Reality*, and my second digression, below).

4 When I snap my fingers you will open your eyes

We find ourselves beside a fire in the lobby of a hotel in Eastbourne. Mr Donaghy has shown us this watch before.

IT IS AN ANCIENT MARINER . . . The illusion of the physical presence of the poet depends on the illusion of the present moment of the poem, a moment in which the poet can assert his or her presence. Look at this watch. If I press this, a spring mechanism flicks open its heavily tarnished gold-plated lid.

Chironomy again. With such modest gestures the poet opens up a little world for the poem.

It's precisely here that the poet creates the illusion of the poem's moment. On a particular day, in a particular room, a poet holds on his palm a particular object:

Timer

Gold survives the fire that's hot enough
to make you ashes in a standard urn.
An envelope of coarse official buff
contains your wedding ring which wouldn't burn.

Dad told me I'd to tell them at St James's
that the ring should go in the incinerator.
That 'eternity' inscribed with both their names is
his surety that they'd be together 'later'.

I signed for the parcelled clothing as the son,
the cardy, apron, pants, bra, dress

the clerk phoned down: 6-8-8-3-1 ?
Has she still her ring on? (Slight pause) Yes!

It's on my warm palm now, your burnished ring.

I feel your ashes, head, arms, breasts, womb, legs
sift through its circle slowly, like that thing
you used to let me watch to time the eggs.

Here Tony Harrison performs a kind of magic trick, transforming, by sleight of hand, his mother's wedding ring into the narrow 'waist' of an egg timer (the tiny domestic descendant of that venerable symbol of mortality, the hourglass). See what he's done? Watch again.

The poem begins in the present tense and the second person, addressed to 'you'. For a split second we may believe he's addressing his reader, or employing a universal 'you' – 'to make one ashes . . .'. But when he shifts back to the immediate past in the second stanza it's clear he's invoking a common convention of the elegiac lyric, permitting us to eavesdrop as he talks to his dead mother. In the third quatrain (for this is a symmetrical poem of four four-line stanzas with two purely visual breaks for dramatic emphasis) he describes how her mortal form was degraded by death, reduced to a parcel of garments and a number. When he asks the clerk if '6-8-8-3-1', formerly Mrs Harrison, is still wearing the ring, he gives us a dramatic stage direction '(Slight pause)'

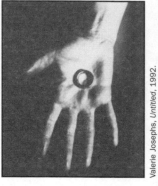

Valerie Josephs, *Untitled*, 1992.

present
past
past
present

in which we're invited to imagine, as the grieving son must, the faceless stranger on the end of the phone line inspecting his mother's naked corpse. And now the sleight of hand: Harrison switches back to the present tense and establishes the imaginary moment of the poem by showing us the object of the poem, the talisman, the ring. But we arrive back at the title by way of a heartbreaking simile, an intimate childhood memory, for the 'timer', not the ring, is the true focus of the son's grief. The ring is inscribed with 'eternity', together with 'surety' the only abstract nouns in the poem, but the timer evokes impermanence. Analysed in this way, Harrison's poem is just so much sideshow trickery, but while we watch his hands he works something akin to true magic. He moves us.

Harrison establishes his poem's enclosure with traditional techniques of rhyme and metre and chiastic structure. Now let's watch another magician, one who uses an altogether different principle of enclosure. Keep your eye on the cup:

The Story of The White Cup
for Helen

I am not sure why I want to tell it
since the cup was not mine and I was not there,
and it may not have been white after all.
When I tell it, though, it is white, and the girl
to whom it has just been given, by her mother,
is eight. She is holding a white cup against her breast,
and her mother has just said goodbye, though those
could not have been, exactly, the words. No one knows
what her father has said, but when I tell it,
he is either helping someone very old with a bag,
a worn valise held in place with a rope,
or asking a guard for a cigarette. There is, of course,

no cigarette. The cattle cars stand with their doors
slid back. They are black inside, and the girl
who has just been given a cup and told to walk
in a straight line and told to look like she wants
a drink of water, who screamed in the truck
all the way to the station, who knew, at eight,
where she was going, is holding a cup to her breast
and walking away, going nowhere, for water.
She does not turn, but when she has found water,
which she does, in all versions of the story, everywhere,
she takes a small sip of it, and swallows.

Here the American poet Roger Mitchell blocks our
habituated emotional responses, our escapes into
historical abstraction, sentimentality, or that media-
generated phenomenon, 'compassion fatigue', by a
formal subterfuge. We can't possibly know where and
when the 'story of the white cup' takes place until
we encounter the words 'cattle cars' – halfway through
the poem, when we're in too deep to back out. Even the
title is strategically misleading, for this is the
story *of the story* of the white cup. Like
Coleridge, Mitchell has interposed a voice
compelled to bear witness, 'I am not sure
why I want to tell it', a formula that might
as easily imply indolence as urgency. The
style is studied artlessness – no similes, no
metaphors, no discernible poetic diction –
but the storyteller must offer us specificity,
focus, or the story evaporates, so he fills in
the gaps 'When I tell it, though, it is white'
informing us at every stage of his decisions:
'but when I tell it, / he is either helping some-
one very old with a bag, / a worn valise held
in place with a rope, / or asking a guard
for a cigarette'. 'Bag', of course, is blurry, so

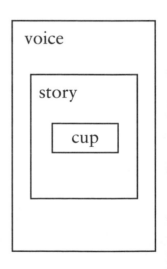

voice

story

cup

he slowly twists his lens to a sharper image, to more information, to the desperation and fear implied by the incongruous 'valise' (US, overnight bag) overpacked and held shut by a rope. But whatever its colour, the one object beyond fabrication is the cup, the talisman at the centre of the story, a story framed by voice, a voice framed by the poem. And it's the cup that locates us in the present of a German or Polish railway station in, say, 1942, in the *presence* of the poem. Because in Mitchell's 'telling' the past tense is transmuted at every point into the present – *I am telling it . . . it is white.*

I defer here to the magus of unsupported assertion, Ezra Pound, who famously defined his version of the image as 'that which presents an intellectual and emotional complex in an instant of time'. That 'instant' reminds me of 'instamatic', and of the documentary truth of the snapshot (and George Eastman had sold his first Brownie only a decade before). A Grecian urn may well represent an 'intellectual and emotional complex', but an 'instant' can focus an allegorical vessel floating in eternity into a teacup in Blooms-bury in 1913. But half a century earlier we can watch another magician use a similar strategy to describe time in spatial terms whilst casually obliterating an oaf with an eagle feather.[14]

---

14. 'The left hemisphere of the brain maps spatial information into a temporal order while the right hemisphere maps temporal information onto a spatial order'. Jerre Levy, quoted by Turner and Pöppel, quoted in *Wallflowers, a lecture on poetry, with misplaced notes and additional heckling,* Michael Donaghy, London 1999. They continue: 'The fact that experienced musicians use their left brain just as much as their right in listening to music shows that their higher understanding of music is the result of the collaboration of both "brains", the music having been translated first from temporal sequence to spatial pattern, and then "read back into a temporal movement"'.

Memorabilia

Ah, did you once see Shelley plain,
And did he stop and speak to you?
And did you speak to him again?
How strange it seems, and new!

But you were living before that,
And you are living after,
And the memory I started at –
My starting moves your laughter!

I crossed a moor, with a name of its own
And a certain use in the world no doubt,
Yet a hand's-breadth of it shines alone
'Mid the blank miles round about:

For there I picked up on the heather
And there I put inside my breast
A moulted feather, an eagle-feather –
Well, I forget the rest.

I'm just as struck by the sheer venom of this little poem as I am by its modernity. Browning is reported to have related 'with characteristic vehemence "I was one day in the shop of Hodgson, the well known London bookseller, when a stranger . . . spoke of something that Shelley had once said to him. Suddenly the stranger paused, and burst into laughter as he observed me staring at him with blanched face . . . I still vividly remember how strangely the presence of a man who had seen and spoken with Shelley affected me"'. The present moment of the poem is represented here by that dash after 'at' in line seven when he interrupts himself – as though he were being interrupted again by the stranger's laughter – and again in line fifteen, before delivering his withering coup de grâce. At which point, I think, we're supposed to imagine Browning, or Browning's stunt man, turning on his heels leaving the speechless recipient contemplating his kinship to a stretch of unremarkable moorland. For that's the principal metaphor of this poem; *time* – an incident in a stranger's life, a few words with the author of 'The Triumph of Life' – equated with *space* – a hand's-breadth of moor occupied by a feather. But we only arrive at this conclusion by way of a secondary equation, when we return to a gesture performed in time, a neume and talisman (forgive me) when Browning slips the feather in his pocket. Pardon me. An *eagle* feather in his *breast*. For these are venerable emblems: the eagle, of power and isolate majesty, the feather, or quill, of the scribe or poet, the breast, of the house of the soul. He has taken this second-hand glimpse of Shelley to his heart. And then?

Nothing. Browning 'forgets the rest' he tells us in the last line of the poem, which, as all good poets know, is the line designed to send the reader's eye back to the title. 'Memorabilia' retains both the mnemonic meaning of rhetorical points or images to be remembered as well as the ordinary sense of the bric-a-brac and relics of fame, and Browning marries both meanings here. The apparent modernity of the poem, Browning's abrupt excursion into the countryside, owes nothing to any theory, programme, or manifesto. It's simply a matter of wit, timing, and performance. 'Sir', he might have said, 'you may have a name, and a use in the world, *no doubt*, but you are clearly not the *subject* of this poem'.

Second digression

Before we go any further it may very well have occurred to you that I've been throwing the words 'subject' and 'object' about with abandon. To clear things up let's check the etymology of these abstract terms. Not surprisingly, they started life as physical actions. 'Object' comes from *objectus*, past participle of *obicere* 'to throw in the way, prevent, hinder', from *ob-* in the way + *jacere* to throw. 'Subject' derives from *subjectus*, pp. of *subicere*, 'to throw under'. No ideas but in neumes, and as the above examples show, all abstraction in language and thought is a system of concrete metaphors unanchored from their roots in the physical world. Even as basic an abstraction as the verb 'to be' is rooted in the Sanskrit *bhu*, 'to grow', whereas 'am' and 'is' share a root with the Sanskrit *asmi*, 'to breathe'.

As a noun, my dictionary defines 'object' as 1) something material that may be perceived by the senses: 'I see an object in the distance'; 2) something mental or physical toward which thought, feeling, or action is directed; 'an object for study' or a 'meticulously carved art object'; and 3) the goal or end of an effort or activity, a purpose, objective.

For 'subject' we have, first, the mind, ego, or agent that sustains thought or consciousness; 2) one that is acted upon; 3) an individual whose reactions or responses are studied; 4) something concerning which something is said or done, 'the subject of the study'; 5) something represented or indicated in a work of art.[15]

---

15. I'd prepared much of the present lecture when I received this e-mail from a friend at the Arts Council whose judgement I respect above my own. [1a]

MD –

Re your essay Wallflowers on poetry and the poetry reader: For my part I find the argument, insofar as it can be classed an argument at all, reasonably accessible. But the style – especially for an oral presentation, is entirely too cluttered. At times I felt I was navigating through some dark dance club packed with gyrating ravers and my friends had gone missing and the strobe lights were hammering away on my retinas. In short, what I had supposed substances were thinned away into shadows, while everywhere shadows were deepened into substances.

Clearly, there's a grey area where the word subject will do as well as object. In becoming art, all objects become subjects, that is, they are mediated – whether represented or merely presented by the consciousness of the poet. The neumes and talismans I see in so many lyric poems, the imaginary moment outside time in which the audience focuses on the poet's hand, and, in that hand, the ring, cup, feather, knife, 'bracelet of bright hair about the bone', the moment in which that talisman becomes a living presence . . . all these have as their precedent the central ritual gesture of European civilization these past two millennia – the elevation of the host in the sacrifice of the Mass.

End of digression

Rest assured, though, that I look forward to your book on Bruno, Coleridge, Yeats and Joyce which you've been threatening to write since 1977. Save the metaphysics for that future project. If you take this direction in the present lecture, the event will extend for several days. And as far as publishing a lecture of such a length . . . well, funds are limited.
Best of luck anyway,
– RJL

I couldn't argue with this, so I'll content myself for the present with sketching the conclusions of a carefully constructed argument which I have reserved for that future publication.

1a. Well, I would.

5 In Lieu of a Conclusion

TIME'S UP. Let me finish, if not conclude, with a few quotable memorabilia. First, twentieth-century literary poetry has been at war with itself and its readers. Secondly, this has not been an unalloyed boon. By attacking traditional terms of engagement with the audience, modernist poets and critics at once cut poetry's lifeline to the oral tradition and developed immeasurably our capacity to think speculatively and innovatively about the genre. But now that the century's up, how do we re-engage with poems?

Memorize. When we learn a dance step, a part in a play, a song, or a poem by heart, we give it a body to live in. We own a poem, or at least our expression of it, in a profoundly deeper way than is possible if it's stored away on a page. But why is this desirable? If poetry is merely a sophisticated cultural toy, or a commodified entertainment, it's a pointless exercise. But if you're reading this essay, chances are you already believe that a great poem is in some sense a repository of wisdom, or wonder, or presence, if only by virtue of its own excellence. If its words are ingrained in our memories they're constantly available to our unconscious, like a computer program running in the background. If its words are inscribed on our hearts, they can guide us out of our emptiness. Time's up.

Readers, I appeal to you! 'Mr Donaghy', as the words on the right insist on calling themselves, is a mirage. These words, however, are entirely your own. Pay no attention to that man behind the curtain!

6 Concluding Neume

In his loneliness and fixedness he yearneth towards the journeying Moon, and the stars that still sojourn, yet still move onward; and every where the blue sky belongs to them, and is their appointed rest, and their native country and their own natural homes, which they enter unannounced, as lords that are certainly expected and yet there is a silent joy at their arrival.

JOHN KEATS holds out his hand:

This living hand, now warm and capable
Of earnest grasping, would, if it were cold
And in the icy silence of the tomb,
So haunt thy days and chill thy dreaming nights
That thou wouldst wish thine own heart dry of blood
So in my veins red life might stream again,
And thou be conscience-calmed – see here it is –
I hold it towards you.

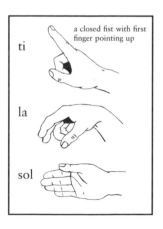

Acknowledgements

Imagine growing up in a society where one's first and only experience of music occurred in a schoolroom, where the beauty of music was meticulously analysed and explained to you and where you were judged by your ability to explain it in turn. In one sense your appreciation of music would be exquisitely sophisticated because tunes wouldn't be tinkling persistently out of lift speakers or commuters' headphones. Music wouldn't be an 'on' switch away, so you'd be more alert to its nuances when you did hear it. But let's face it, you wouldn't be queuing round the corner for the experience. It would always be more 'improving' than pleasurable. Well that's more or less our (urban, educated, Anglophone) experience of poetry. Perhaps its low profile has to do with the way it's taught. On the graduate level, modern pedagogues have long felt disinclined to lead tour groups around the gallery waving their pointing sticks at the sheer genius of the Old Masters. They want to be the main event. Literacy corrupts, they seem to be saying, and Literature, the common ground of writing agreed to be worthy of survival, is the tool of the oppressor. If poetry depended on intellectuals for its survival it would be about as current as hieroglyphics.

They exhibit common scholarly errors of reading from the outside, of treating the 'canon' as a corpse to be wheeled out for dissection practice by generations of medical students. Literary taste was effectively banished from the curriculum when I was a student. I remember complaining that a particular contemporary poet we were studying wasn't to my taste. The professor looked baffled. 'Taste?' He laughed and pointed to his tongue. 'Taste is here.' I was pleasantly surprised when another professor – James K. Chandler – read Coleridge's 'Frost at Midnight' aloud, all 567 words of it, paused, and asked us if we thought it was beautiful. Thanks, Jim. That's the only time in my experience of academe I got any indication that it might be relevant to find pleasure in a poem.

For the past year I've been 'reader-in-residence' for the Poetry Society. I tried the opposite approach, running discussions and 'close readings' of poems, mostly with groups of librarians, in which we tried to understand the poem from a maker's point of view. In other words, I followed the example set by schools of music and painting, where criticism and theory are taught in conjunction with practice. If your only experience of motoring lay in deconstructing the Highway Code you could hardly be expected to understand the allure of the automobile, so I took my readers for a spin round the block.

MICHAEL DONAGHY

CRITICISM AND REVIEWS

T. S. Eliot

Inventions of the March Hare, Poems 1909–1917

Imagine a digitally remastered CD of all the mistakes Alfred Brendel made when he was learning the piano, or the telephone doodling pads of Francis Bacon printed with an exhaustive commentary by Brian Sewell. Such exercises, I hear you say, can only be of interest to the pathologically obsessive fan or, worse, the professionally obsessive academic. Faber's publication of *Inventions of the March Hare, Poems 1909–1917*, a collection of Eliot's previously unpublished early verse edited by Christopher Ricks, appears to be targeted at the latter category.

In 1922, just before *The Waste Land* was published, Eliot offered the American lawyer John Quinn the ms, which Quinn accepted only on condition Eliot sell him a second ms – the notebook in question – for $140. Eliot dismissed the notebook as 'a great many sets of verse which never have been printed and which I am sure you will agree never ought to be printed, and in putting them in your hands, *I beg you fervently to keep them to yourself and see that they are never printed.*' (My italics.) After Quinn's death Eliot assumed the poems were safely dead and buried. But here they are after seventy years, some twenty 'new' poems written between 1909 and 1911, the same period in which Eliot also composed 'The Love Song of J. Alfred Prufrock', 'Portrait of a Lady', and 'Preludes'. The newly exhumed verse will have at least one unquestionably positive effect on ordinary readers – most of it's so wretched that they will be forced to reassess the poems upon which the great man's reputation rests. Rest assured the foundation stands.

As one might expect, much of this embarrassing stuff sounds like the work of a 'Prufrock'-besotted undergraduate: 'O danse mon papillon noir! / Within the circle of my brain? / The twisted dance continues' or 'to hear my Madness singing, sitting on the kerbstone / a blind old drunken man who sings and mutters, / With broken boot heels stained in many gutters' or 'Then I have gone at night through narrow streets, / Where evil houses leaning all together / Pointed a ribald finger at me in the darkness'. The volume also contains some pages of bawdy verse which offer some relief, because this, at least, we can be sure he never took seriously.

In his annotations Professor Ricks has accomplished something positively Herculean. For *half the volume's length* he glosses every possible literary intimation and very many highly improbable ones – the poems themselves are sandwiched in between pages 11 and 93 – but perhaps this is an appropriate response to the one poet we associate above all others with the cut-and-paste method of intertextual allusion. 'The poet's mind', Eliot was later to write in *Tradition and the Individual Talent*, 'is a receptacle for seizing and storing up numberless feelings, phrases, images, which remain there until all the particles which unite to form a new compound are present together.' This book urges us to consider the precisions of that statement – the poet appropriates *feelings* as well as phrases – and much of the effect of the early poems derives from the suspicion that any given phrase might be nicked from Tennyson or Webster and any emotion from the etiolated dandyism of Laforgue. Not that you can blame the twentysomething Eliot for his adolescent weariness with life, and surely he deserves some credit for all but throwing them away.

This publication arrives in the wake of the recent furore over Anthony Julius's *T. S. Eliot, Anti-Semitism and Literary Form*. But the issue of Eliot's anti-Semitism is relevant here as only one facet of the modernist personality exemplified by Hulme, Lewis, Pound, and Eliot. It is part of a cultural complex that appears to have included a schoolboy misogyny and proto-fascism. Anti-Semitism was part of the atmosphere in the London of 1909, and Eliot's share of it could only have been focused by his association with Pound and Lewis, who associated Jews with bodily fluids and odours and with bodily infection. Far more apparent in these early poems is Eliot's contempt for the working class and particularly his fascinated disgust with women: they are neurotic coquettes or shopgirls who would never know what to wear to the opera or who 'smile through false teeth'; housemaids have crimson fists, emerge 'spilling out of corsets' or else they display laughable attempts to appropriate culture, as in 'Afternoon': 'The ladies who are interested in Assyrian art / Gather in the hall of the British Museum. / The faint perfume of last year's tailor suits / And the steam from drying rubber overshoes / And the green and purple feathers on their hats / Vanish in the sombre Sunday afternoon'. How ridiculous! Imagine approaching Culture in rubber overshoes! Like Prufrock's women who 'come and go / Talking of Michelangelo' they only distract the poet briefly before they 'fade beyond the Roman statuary / Like amateur comedians across a lawn' ('There is no doubt that in our headlong rush to educate everybody, we are lowering our standards' Eliot was later to write in *Christianity and Culture*). Throughout the writings of Lewis, Hulme, Pound, and Eliot one discovers this pathological concern with 'hard, clear outlines', 'muscularity' and 'dryness' which they regarded as classical or 'masculine' qualities, and a congruent aversion to the 'feminine' qualities of 'slush' and 'sentiment' (i.e. emotion). A look at Eliot's juvenilia confirms that these tastes proceed from something deeper than intellectual conviction.

Should you buy this book? It depends. Because of Professor Ricks's commodious annotations, the scholarly mills can stay open, and the working poet can probably benefit from a closer inspection of Eliot's methods, but the ordinary reader will have to shell out £30 to read a handful of poems that range from the promising to the perfectly appalling.

John Updike

RABBITINGS

Collected Poems

At his best, John Updike spins a humane, exuberant musical rhetoric from a metaphysical junkheap of bicycle chains, telephone poles, the erection, and the Resurrection. His *Collected Poems* is replete with stunningly wrought lines and startling metaphors. 'The Angels', for example, are the great artists and composers who continually remind us that there is a realm 'above this plane of silent compromise'. Above and below, they surround us 'echoing in subway tunnels, / springing like winter flowers from postcards / Scotch-taped to white kitchen walls . . . burning in memory like leaky furnace doors'. Here he balances passion and wit so adroitly that he earns the rhetorical grandeur of the ending: 'Love us, dead Thrones: / sing us to sleep, awaken our eyes, / comfort with terror our mortal afternoons.'

But when Updike nods, he snores. His badness, like his sexism, requires a separate study. It's troubling to encounter a writer of Updike's intelligence unable, or unwilling, to distinguish between his best work and his mistakes. More troubling still are the poems that almost made it before the skill took over. For when it comes to the alchemical payoff, when it comes, in short, to the poetry, John Updike rarely bothers.

For the most part, he's cheerfully and graciously aware of this; almost a third of the volume is devoted to light verse, a genre which died off in America, he once remarked, at about the same time dancers in movies stopped going up and down stairs in white tie and tails. In his own light verse he 'strings some similar [sic] things, French inventors, semi-extinct animals, new developments in particle physics, in a kind of necklace of stanzas and steps back pleased.'

This *bijouterie* is a hallmark of his style, which begs an awkward question: How does he *know* when he's writing light verse? Unfortunately, he has a formula. A real poem, he tells us in the book's Preface, 'derives from the real (the given, the substantial) world and light verse from the man-made world of information – books, newspapers, words, signs . . . a number of entries wavered back and forth across the border.' Most of the book, in fact. Often, the effect is a waste of talent and energy: Fred Astaire attempting to dance 'The Rite of Spring'.

Many of the poems feel like alarmingly successful workshop exercises, each hurtling toward its closure like a door slamming: Updike contemplating a windowframe, a stalk of celery, a blowjob. He demonstrates the ease of a Major League pitcher as he lobs us his processed subjects. Here, try this golfball. This wristwatch. I ducked at 'The Beautiful Bowel Movement' ('O spiral Perfection, not seashell nor / stardust, how can I keep you? With this poem'). Was there ever a more brazen case of Cheating the Hangman?

For some poets the enterprise of writing poetry begins with momentarily forgetting that it's impossible. But for a Method poet like Updike, it's simply a matter of sticking to the formula. Consider the Augustan poets who had only to flesh out ideas in poetic diction and dress them up as nymphs and shepherds. Grainger's or Cowley's elaborate scientific allegories in rhyme are perfectly logical, perfectly ridiculous, perfectly tasteless.

Updike, of course, knows he's being tasteless. He aspires to it. Cowley is to Updike what Shakespeare was to Keats. He even shares with the great James Grainger a poem on rats. 'The villains pass / with scrabbly traffic noise . . .' (Updike); 'the whiskered vermin race' (Grainger). And 'Seven Odes To Natural Processes' ploughs remorselessly through Entropy, Crystallization, Evaporation etc. for fourteen pages.

'Midpoint' also invokes Augustan mannerism among its many styles (which include photographs from a family album and a cod concretism). It's an ambitious sprawl of a poem but Updike sabotages it with his patented porno-kitsch. In a section where he 'addresses those he has loved' individual women blur into Woman:

> you whose breast I soaped
> and you my cock, and your cunt
> indivisible from the lather and huge as a purse and the
> mirror giving us back ourselves . . .
>
> . . . and in the Caribbean the night you knelt
> to be taken from behind and we were entangled
> with the mosquito netting
> and in the woods you let me hold your breasts
> your lipstick all flecked
> the twigs dissolved in the sky above and I jerked off
> driving home alone one-handed
> singing of you.

Object that Updike is not writing – or driving – with due care and attention and he defiantly stares you down, flashing his ironic licence. Taste?

> I have, alas, no taste –
> taste, that Talleyrand, that ally of the minimal,
> that foreign-accented intuiter . . .

He concludes 'Taste' by rolling up his sleeves and slapping Nature on the back: 'I want to be like Nature, tasteless, abundant, reckless, cheerful.' Which is cheating, of course. Updike displays more than enough intuition (i.e. tastes) to craft a real poem, but that, he seems to say, would be downright UnAmerican. Believe me, if he weren't so busy being reckless, abundant, and cheerful, he might have produced a smaller but weightier collection. His light verse, I should add, is often quite funny.

Boris Pasternak

Boris Pasternak
Peter Levi

Second Nature, Forty-Six Poems
Boris Pasternak, trans. Andrei Navrozov

Poems 1955–1959 and An Essay in Autobiography
Boris Pasternak, trans. Michael Harari and Manya Harari

The Western estimate of Boris Pasternak resembles nothing so much as a novel based on the life of an imaginary artist. So says Andrei Navrozov in the introduction to his translations of forty-six Pasternak poems, but the artist he proposes is not, as you might expect, Zhivago, but Anton Leverkuhn, the composer hero of Mann's *Doctor Faustus*. It's an apt comparison: translations of poems are never more than descriptions and without Russian we can no more get at the essence of Pasternak's poetry than hear Leverkuhn's music. Nevertheless, Navrozov, who knows these verses by heart, does his best to convey the elusive tone and rich music of the originals. But can the tone survive the music? All those double rhymes jangle terribly in English: 'Now winking, now twinkling, now quietly sleeping! / The beloved, asleep, fairy visions unravels. / Meanwhile, the heart, like a coupling keeps leaping, / Scattering sparks through the plain in its travels'. Based on versions like these, it's difficult to credit Mandelstam's claim that Pasternak was 'the initiator of a new mode of prosody commensurate with the maturity and virility of the Russian language.'

In his lively and sympathetic biography Peter Levi employs a variety of translations, his own, Robert Lowell's, and John Stall-worthy's. Here is his own rendering of the same stanza: 'They wink, they blink, and yet sweetly somewhere / My love like a mirage and others sleep / While the heart splashes along carriage footboards / Scattering bright windows over the steppe.' Less rhythmical, perhaps, but considerably more believable. I would have preferred an unrhymed version, but Levi can't resist flexing his technical muscle. In demonstrating the accuracy of Pasternak's translations of Shakespeare, for example, he renders the Russian back into English ('Her boat burned on the waters like the globe, / the stern of it was golden, and the sail / was purple, some sweet fragrance burnt on it, / and the wind died away in ecstasy.')

Poems 1955–1959 offers the original text on the facing page, and Michael Harari's spare, colloquial translations respect Pasternak's own principle that the poem must conform to what one might actually say. But – as in *Zhivago* – the poems themselves are only a part of the story. They are overshadowed by a mythological giant called Boris Pasternak.

How did he survive the Stalin era? If we are to believe Levi, he got by on a curious combination of other-worldiness and guile. His Pasternak is an innocent wandering relatively unscathed for twenty years through the eye of a political hurricane. Rather than sign a public declaration of mourning when Stalin's wife committed suicide in 1932, he sent a personal note of condolence and Levi notes that for the next twenty years his police file bore a mark protecting him from arrest. Furthermore, his decision to translate the Georgian poets undoubtedly appealed to the great Georgian himself, who found Pasternak's unshakeable hieratic optimism unthreatening and duly appointed him to the governing boards of the new Union of Writers. 'I could have written any filth or trash', he complained bitterly, 'and they would have published it.' It seems that he became Stalin's pet poet in spite of himself, and his immunity must have been a leaden weight on his conscience.

Shortly after the publication of *Doctor Zhivago* in 1957 he was summoned by the Union of Writers; 'I'm in for trouble this time,' he told a friend, 'my turn has come.' The following year he was awarded the Nobel Prize. There's no doubt that the furious reaction of the authorities, the betrayals by old friends and public denunciations broke and finally killed him. But on a deeper level, perhaps, they were his long-awaited absolution.

C. K. Williams

THE LIBERAL LINE

Collected Poems 1963–85
Bloodaxe

Flesh and Blood
Bloodaxe

For several years now American poetry has felt the insistent influence of its most ambitious and original talent since mid-century. C. K. Williams began his career in the radical atmosphere of sixties America, a radicalism fuelled by opposition to the Vietnam War. Reading his work of that period I was constantly reminded of the rage and disgrace felt by American poets of my generation. I was also reminded of how shrill and incoherent some of our poetry was, as if the conventions of grammar and syntax – let alone rhyme and metre – were somehow in league with Kissinger and General Motors. It was a period when, as the American poet Alan Shapiro recalls, form and technique were equated with rationality and repression and experimental verse with emotional and political liberation. As a result, much of what was intended to be resistance poetry turned out to be merely resistant.

Williams' second book, *I Am The Bitter Name* (1971), exhibits a marked degree of this derangement; he even dispenses with the bourgeois frippery of punctuation. At one point, he describes the sense of urgency which lay behind what now seems like pointless experimentation: '. . . *I'm working as fast as I can I can't stop to use periods / sometimes I draw straight lines on the page because the words are too slow*' ('Yours'). Nevertheless, it's a commendable effort, partly because Williams' compassion and rage for order inform his rage at Johnson and Nixon, and if the result isn't always great poetry, we are left with the impression of a great moral intelligence confronting profound personal and political evil.

He fulfils his promise in his third book, *With Ignorance* (1977), and it's here that he adopts the line of roughly ten metrical feet which makes his current work immediately recognizable on the page. Visually, this amplified free verse may remind us of earlier practitioners of the 'American long line', of Whitman or Ginsberg – until we start to read them and find an altogether more complex sensibility at work. Take the astonishingly beautiful poem from the 1983 volume *Tar*, 'My Mother's Lips':

> Until I asked her to please stop doing it and was astonished to
>   find that she not only could
> but from the moment I asked her would stop doing it, my
>   mother, all through my childhood,
> when I was saying something to her, something important,
>   would move her lips as I was speaking
> so that she seemed to be saying under her breath the very words
>   I was saying as I was saying them

It's only later, when his own children are learning to talk, that he recognizes the parental urge to 'lift you again from those blank caverns of namelessness we encase'. After this initial epiphany the narrative folds back on itself:

> That was long afterward, though: where I was right now was
>   just wanting to get her to stop
> And considering how I brooded and raged in those days, how
>   quickly my teeth went on edge
> The restraint I approached her with seems remarkable, although
>   her so unprotestingly,
> Readily taming a habit by then three children and a dozen years
>   old was as much so.

The power of this technique lies in our different expectations for verse and prose. On the one hand, we are offered a 'prosy' grammatical sentence, but the derangement of the early work is still there, driving it into verse. In fact, it takes more than one reading just to extract the grammatical structure of this sentence from behind the interpolated clauses. What it requires, and ultimately suggests, are the tonal modulations, which is to say the music, of a speaking voice; specifically, a liberal, analytical voice. And Williams seeks to render its music as it examines its motives, considers its alternatives, and refines its meanings. The dithyrambs of Whitman and Jeffers and the Beats are not conducive to reconsideration or self-doubt: the 'open shirted buddies of the universe' – as a friend of mine once called them – always seem to be shouting at us from the heights of enlightenment. What Williams has to tell us of love and pity is far more intimate and convincing.

No, the precedent that springs to mind is not Whitman, but the quieter and more subversive Wordsworth of *Lyrical Ballads*: the poet as young radical trying to forge a moral and political *instrument* out of poetic diction and description. The constant interruptions and emotional fine-tunings are strategic; they're meant to impede our rush to judgement – look again. Think again. At a conference last year Williams criticized the privileged status accorded to emotion in America's 'psychotherapeutic' culture. Emotions, he said, 'are in and of themselves neither pure, spontaneous, nor very clear. They require a stringent attentiveness, and, if the soul is to do justice to their turbulence and furore without belittling itself, it must be educated, and rigorously so'. For Williams, poetry is the soul's best tutor. Perhaps 'stringent attentiveness' is his 'wise passiveness'.

In fact, when I hear the usual objections to Williams I think of the famous *Preface*: 'They who have been accustomed to the gaudiness and inane phraseology of modern writers will, no doubt, frequently have to struggle with feelings of awkwardness and confusion'. Where's the lapidary concision? Where's the daffy surrealism? The knee-jerk ironies? The dramatic monologues? Williams occupies a different poetic universe, a universe in which attention (to each other, to what we read, feel and see) is the cardinal virtue. Neglect is the cardinal sin. It results in the almost unreadable squalor and degradation he seeks to redeem through his exacting, vivid descriptions of crippled Vietnam vets, pornographic models, suicides, and lunatics (the equivalent of Wordsworth's vagrants and leech-gatherers). Be warned. We're spared nothing, not even the evacuations of a diseased dog: '. . . the feeble, mucus-coated, blood-flecked chains that finally spurted from him' ('The Dog'). But the beauty he wrests from oblivion is all the sweeter for being hard won.

The same attentiveness leads Williams to violate one of the great taboos of creative writing: he is not shy around adjectives. In fact, he packs them in, before and after the noun, in staccato bursts. Sunlight is 'oblique, relentless, unadorned', and the clouds are 'dense, low, irregular'. He also breaks a corollary law which can be summed up in Pound's dictum 'Go in fear of abstractions'. Shifting abruptly from sensory description to a no less rigorous observation of ideas and emotions, he represents an overdue reaction to the other Williams's catchy injunction, 'No ideas but in things'. Indeed, in 'One of The Muses', the long poem which concludes *Tar*, 'things' don't even put in an appearance. It's the record of a mental breakdown, an interior odyssey, expressed, at times, in terms of prosody: 'I tried to reconceive myself, to situate myself in the syntax of our cripped sentence. / I parsed myself, searching out a different flow for the tangle of amputated phrases I was by then. / Nothing, though, would sound, would scan, no matter how I carved, dissected, chopped'.

I suspect 'One Of The Muses' belongs to the same genre as Blake's prophetic books, an allegorical narrative in which all the parts are played by carefully distinguished spiritual forces. And at one point in the poem a palpable 'new mind', with ideas similar to Blake's comes upon him very much in the same way that the spirit of the poet enters Blake's foot in *Milton*: 'My new mind comes upon me with a hush, a fluttering, a silvery ado, and it has a volume / granular and sensitive, which exactly fits the volume of the mind I already have'. It's hard to imagine staying up with a poet for sixteen pages of psychological turmoil unrelieved by a single reference to the natural world. But, remarkably, 'One Of The Muses' commands our attention and leaves us breathless.

It's a curious paradox that an artist's imagination is often freed by seemingly arbitrary technical constraints. Maybe it's because the unconscious only kicks into gear when the conscious mind is busy negotiating wit the form. One man's I Ching is another man's sestina. In his new collection, *Flesh And Blood*, Williams adheres strictly to an eight-line form with brilliant results. This is the same conversational free-verse line, but now the wide-ranging romantic narratives of the last two books are delimited and compressed into luminous, sonnet-sized epiphanies. And it's funnier. Never lightweight, mind you, but he has at last achieved the confidence to smile from time to time:

> The father has given his year-old son *Le Monde* to play with in
>   his stroller and the baby does
> just what you'd expect: grabs it, holds it out in front of him,
>   stares importantly at it,
> makes emphatic and dramatic sounds of declamation, great
>   pronouncements of analytic probity,
> then tears it, pulls a page in half, pulls the half in quarters,
>   shoves a hearty shred in his mouth –

('Reading: Early Sorrow')

I'll resist the temptation to quibble over the fine points of this collection. The fine points are a matter of taste, and any really important poet will challenge your taste. By and large these poems surprise and convince us, and ultimately we're moved by the serious status Williams accords to poetry. Buy these books and let them go to work on you.

Richard Wilbur

DEFENSIBLE POSITIONS

*'Every poem begins, or ought to,
by a disorderly retreat to defensible positions.'*
R.W.

With Faber's publication of Richard Wilbur's *New and Collected Poems* comes the opportunity to reappraise the work of that graceful lyricist who has experienced the most widely fluctuating reputation of any living American poet. Initially he was borne aloft by the orthodoxies of postwar criticism. Through the fifties American poetry was supported by academic approval and most of the New Critics were themselves poets. Although these elegant craftsmen paid lip service to modernism they were anxious to get the rough beast buried; understandably, considering the political record of the modernists. 'Tradition' offered an escape from ideology.

Inevitably, the next generation prepared to murder its symbolic fathers. Along came Donald Allen's *The New American Poetry* and Wilbur's stock plummeted. One of the dimmer beacons of American Lit. Crit., Leslie Feidler complained that he found in Wilbur 'no personal source anywhere, as there is no passion and no insanity . . .' What? No insanity? This was 1964, mind you, when exhibitionism and suicide were the advisable routes to anthologized respectability, and here was a perfectly sane man with the effrontery to call himself a poet!

But now, almost thirty years on, with a spirit of detente between the factions, it's worth considering why Wilbur never played the confessional card. He began writing poems in 1943 as 'a momentary stay against confusion' while on active service with the 36th Infantry Division. Having experienced Monte Cassino, Anzio and the Siegfried Line firsthand he must have been rather unimpressed by the next generation's production of private hells. His decisions to eschew the confessional 'I', to write in rhyme and metre, were moral decisions, civic, and militantly liberal.

During the Vietnam War Wilbur contributed little to the available stock of protest poetry. He knew that overtly political verse is almost always an exercise in preaching to the converted, so he did just that. 'For the Student Strikers' begins 'Go talk with those who are rumored to be unlike you / And whom, it is said, you are so unlike / Stand on the stoops of their houses and tell them why / You are out on strike'. It's not one of Wilbur's best poems, but I wonder who the most profitably engaged poets of this time really were – Wilbur urging the student strikers to cultivate grassroots support for the peace movement, or Robert Bly dancing about in his poncho intoning 'The Teeth Mother Naked At Last'.

But there's a final, overriding reason why a Wilbur revival is long overdue; he has a perfect ear, perhaps the most flawless command of musical phrase of any American poet. If only for the technique, every poet ought to own and study this book.

Timothy Steele

RHYME CRIME USA

Missing Measures:
Modern Poetry and the Revolt against Meter

Expansive Poetry:
Essays on the New Narrative and the New Formalism,
Edited by Frederick Feirstein

The burning issue in American poetry today is the war between those who write rhymed, metrical, or at least narrative verse, and just about everyone who doesn't. It is a tempest in an enormous, expensive teacup.

But there's a twist in the latest conflict. Last time round the established poets were scholars and critics and the challenge came from the beats and confessionals. Today, those rebels all chair creative writing departments and condemn the carefully wrought lyrics written off-campus by psychologists, novelists, feminist philosophers, and business executives.

But just why is it that every few years the same battle lines are drawn up between modern and romantic, raw and cooked, beat and square, redskin and paleface? And why is this stylistic issue always expressed in the crudest caricature of politics? Given that *vers libre* was an elite mode initiated by the extreme right, it seems strange that so many American poets equate irregular line lengths with democracy. I believe the key to this puzzle lies in America's cultural inferiority complex. The fact that the history of literature in English is mostly English makes American poets defensive. In a 1986 issue of *Poetry East* devoted to Poetics, for example, Louis Simpson says the English favour metrical verse because they have 'prejudices rather than principles' whereas.

> I think there is also a basis [for free verse] in our political philosophy, our preference for democracy – moving from the particular to the general, rather than submitting to some form of centralized power, though I am not able to prove this . . .

No prejudice *there*. 'Americans', he continues, 'don't have an ear for meter and rhyme . . . Our thoughts don't move in meter or sound in rhyme'. Lucky for him. I always have to translate mine into prose. Elsewhere, a bizarrely xenophobic Diane Wakowski warns that American formal poets threaten 'the free verse revolution, and . . . the poetry which is the fulfilment of the Whitman heritage'. She even calls Frost a closet European on account of his facility with traditional rhythms. Formalist Dana Gioia observed rather acutely that Wakowski's remarks 'seem curiously reminiscent in tone and content to the quest for pure Germanic culture led by the late Joseph Goebbels'.

Out of all this journalistic fray has emerged at least one scholarly, if partisan, history of the debate by one of the best New Formalist poets. Timothy Steele's *Missing Measures* is not a manifesto. In fact, he never mentions the movement or any of its disciples and he obviously admires the scope and ambition of the modernist enterprise. However, he argues that that enterprise – the 'free verse revolution' celebrated by Wakowski and Co. – failed to achieve its stated aims.

As early as 1918 Pound complained in 'Retrospect' that free verse 'has become as prolix and as verbose as any of the flaccid varieties that preceded it . . . I do not think one can use to any advantage rhythms much more tenuous and imperceptible than some I have used'. And in 1932 W. C. Williams characterized the poetic scene as a 'formless interim', a transitional stage, a kind of testing ground for the prosody of tomorrow.

Steele contends that this new universal metric failed to materialize and a generation of poets tinkered about like Esperanto enthusiasts with one eccentric scheme or system after another: 'composition by field', 'projective verse', and that shoe salesman's nightmare, 'the variable foot'.

Throughout, Steele treats free verse as an anomalous growth caused by a coincidence of errors. He blames the Renaissance confusion of Aristotle's *Poetics* with Quintillian, Servius and Plutarch for the notion that imitation is more central to poetry than verse, that poetry is something *other* than verse. He blames Kantian aestheticism with its stress on the autonomy of the poem ('the inner unity which is unique to every poem', as Eliot said, 'against the outer unity which is typical') for the notion that every poem scans according to its own rules. Music, as the most autonomous, least materialist of the arts, could be elevated as pure expression by an aesthete like Pater, for whom 'all art constantly aspires to the condition of music', so the leaders of the free verse movement almost always described their medium in these terms. Hence Pound's famous injunction to 'compose in the sequence of the musical phrase, not in the sequence of the metronome'. (What on earth did that man think metronomes were *for*? I've always wondered why Dolmetsch, say, didn't take him aside and explain that a musical phrase is based on reproducible rhythms.)

Why did the modernists find traditional prosody so oppressive? Steele illustrates by quoting Ford Madox Ford's lecture on *vers libre*. Ford tells how, as a child, he was forced to attend drawing-room readings by the Brownings and Rossettis. When they began to recite

> the most horrible changes came over these normally nice people . . . they held their heads at unnatural angles and appeared to be suffering the tortures of agonising souls. It was their voices that did that. They were doing what Tennyson calls, with admiration, 'Mouthing out their hollow O's and A's'.

The Victorian method of reading aloud, in other words, was a more regular version of the same artificial sing-song style employed by many contemporary American poets – Steele blames the nineteenth-century schoolroom practice of teaching prosody by monotonously chanting regular stresses ('Thou *still* unr*av*ished *bride* of *quietness*'). Small wonder then that Pound sought to break the pentameter. His mistake, says Steele, lay in confusing fustian Victorian diction and subject matter with the meter in which it was written.

Furthermore, Steele argues, Ford, Eliot, and Pound wanted to win back for poetry a readership that had defected to the novel, an impulse shared by today's American formalists Vikram Seth (Indian by birth but largely an American in *The Golden Gate*) and Marilyn Hacker, who have responded by writing narrative verse rather than surrendering to prose rhythms. Not surprisingly, says Steele, Pound's maxim that verse must be 'at least as well written as prose' transmuted into a notion that verse might be better off written like the novel, without meter.

Missing Measures also gathers together ample evidence to question the 'experimental' and 'revolutionary' pose of the contemporary artist – terms misappropriated from hard science and harder politics. The only truly revolutionary art, of course, would incite revolution, but the American avant garde belong to the culture of advertising, where 'revolutionary' can describe toothpaste. The only true experiments in art are conducted in laboratories on suspect Vermeers, but innumerable poets firmly believe they're engaged in a perpetual, inconclusive research project.

The early modernists believed that in order for art to have a place in modern culture it has to compete with science, to experiment, to produce 'breakthroughs' and contribute to 'progress'. Steele reviews the various modernist poetic briefs and manifestos which were based on popular misinterpretations of the arcane mathematics of the theory of relativity and the Heisenberg uncertainty principle. W. C. Williams, for example, was among the first to enlist Professor Einstein in the free verse revolution: 'It may seem presumptive to state that [free verse] could be an indication of discoveries in the relativity of our measurements of physical matter', he wrote to a contemporary, '. . . but such is the fact'.

Even today American poets often reach for the jargon of quarks and fractals to validate their poetics, though their grasp invariably falls rather short of *Omni* magazine. I find Alice Fulton, for example, in the aforementioned issue of *Poetry East*, enlisting chaos theory as a model for free verse: 'Perhaps popular literature and culture have made people aware of this and other quantum theories such as the view that reality consists of a steadily increasing number of parallel universes; that consciousness creates reality' – one of Mr Spock's quantum theories, no doubt. 'A truly engaged and contemporary poetry', she warns, 'must reflect this knowledge'. A kind of chaos practice, in other words, to reflect chaos theory.

Oddly enough, there's a counter-revolutionary claim to scientific legitimacy that makes these boffins look like trainee phrenologists. *The Neural Lyre* is a bizarre and wonderful collaboration between New Formalist poet Frederick Turner and scientist Ernst Pöppel which is featured in the *real* New Formalist manifesto, a collection of essays called *Expansive Poetry*. Turner and Pöppel claim nothing less than a vindication of regular poetic meter in terms of brain physiology! Based on recent discoveries in human cortical information-processing that the left hemisphere of the brain maps spatial information onto a temporal order while the right hemisphere maps temporal information onto a spatial order, they argue that meter is in part a way of introducing right-brain processes into the left-brain activity of understanding language. Furthermore, they say, the brain possesses an auditory information 'buffer' of three seconds' worth of information, and that this corresponds to a culturally universal and fundamental unit of metered poetry they call a LINE. In all the world's poetry, from Japanese to Ndembu (Zambia) to English, this unit falls within a 2.20 to 3 second cognitive cycle. (Miroslav Holub also cited Turner and Pöppel's work in the title essay of his collection *The Dimension of The Present Moment*, Faber, 1990.)

Having allowed my subscription to *Neuropsychologia* to lapse, I don't feel qualified to challenge the data by which they claim to have proven all this, but, as the physicists say, it's a beautiful system. At the very least, Turner and Pöppel have contributed another masterpiece to the great eccentric tradition of *The White Goddess* and Poe's *Eureka*.

One finds in Dana Gioia a more pragmatic approach. He writes in both free and formal modes because 'Working in free verse helped keep the language of my poems varied and contemporary, just as writing in form helped keep my free verse more focussed and precise'. Gioia represents the reasonable end of the movement, and I look forward to his forthcoming collection of critical essays. But for now the extreme positions adopted by Steele, Turner and Pöppel stand as a corrective to the orthodoxy that made it a crime to rhyme in the USA.

A Letter to Ian Duhig about Timothy Steele

Dear Ian,

I had to laugh out loud when I got your letter this morning because I'd just dropped an enthusiastic review of Steele's book in the post the night before!

Unfortunately, I almost never look at PN Review. I wish I'd seen your response to Chris McCully's review sooner because you pinpoint some real flaws in the book (such as Steele's confusion over who the modernists were and his equation of free verse with modernism).

Nevertheless, I think you've misread Steele on a couple of points. First, the book is intended to slap the American poetry establishment in the face, hence the polemical (or 'fanatical') tone. Everytime Steele mentions the political record of the modernists he does so to disrupt the accepted American notion that form is a European anachronism tainted with reactionary politics. This is why he always qualifies his remarks; he wants to take politics out of the picture altogether.

Second, he states very clearly in his introduction (on page 25) that he admires the modernist enterprise, its 'devotion to poetry' and its 'admirable vitality'. If he doesn't quote much poetry from Eliot and Pound I think it's because he has no argument with their undeniably powerful work – only with the theory. Also, it's worth noting that contemporary American free verse poets don't look to the King James Psalms, James Macpherson, Salomon Gessner, Martin Farquhar Tupper, or even Whitman as the antecedents of American free verse. They believe Pound and Eliot invented the kind of poetry they write.

I have to sympathize with Steele the poet, by the way, however dogmatic he appears as a critic. For years I had to defend my occasional use of rhyme and metre against the STUPIDEST arguments from unbearably arrogant poets, teachers, and editors, who never read anything but American free verse. These people have had positions of power in the American literary scene for almost forty years. Perhaps this situation explains the undercurrent of 'loathing' you correctly detect in Steele's book.

All the best,

New Formalism

CRASHING THE DEVIL'S PARTY

Rebel Angels: 25 Poets of the New Formalism
Edited by Mark Jarman and David Mason, Story Line Press

Looking for convoluted tribal hierarchies, kinship rituals, and creation myths? Why parachute into some unhygienic rainforest when the culture of American poetry is an anthropologist's Disneyland? Here, segregated into traditions of the Raw, under the totem of Whitman, and the Cooked, under Dickinson, almost every poet declares an allegiance to his or her tribe or 'movement'. In Britain a group of poets could once afford to call themselves simply *the* Movement. But in America poets survive, courtesy of the university syllabus, insofar as they can be grouped under headings like 'The New York School', 'Beats', 'Confessionals', 'Objectivists' ('You must have a movement', Harriet Monroe warned a reluctant Louis Zukovsky, 'Give it a name'). A loner hasn't much chance in this game. The best way to pass your poetic genes on to the next generation is to get yourself classified, ranked, and anthologized.

This looks a serviceable anthology for next year's seminar: *Rebel Angels* – a crimson book jacket adorned with a suitably intense image from Blake – *The Good and Evil Angels Struggling for Possession of a Child*. You'd be forgiven for thinking it some wild raw-word salad tossed up by Iain Sinclair. Except that it's full of sonnets. These are what editors Jarman and Mason consider the best of New Formalism, a movement christened, like many literary and artistic movements of the past, by its opponents. If that's not confusing enough, consider the title of the book in relation to the cover illustration. Surely the rebel angels are Satan's Legions, and in Blake's picture it's the evil angel who is losing possession of the child (the public? the Academy? the point?). Just who do these angels think they are?

For all their striking differences, both New Formalism and Language poetry emerged in eighties America as formalist reactions to the typical magazine or writing-program verse of the period – a brief free verse confessional lyric of the sort promoted by the writing programs. In their preface, Jarman and Mason sketch out the background. They recount the explosion of spleen when New Formalism was first acknowledged as a movement around 1985 and the teaching poets rallied round to condemn the upstarts. If one agrees with Valéry that one of the chief pleasures of rhyme is the rage it inspires in its opponents, these attacks make for a diverting read. But how to account for the peculiar intensity of this rage?

It's hard to imagine America's literary inferiority complex before the advent of modernism, now that the roles are reversed and America the dominant world culture. But it fuelled Whitman's campaign to free American literary language from 'the burden of the past' (England, in this context), a task resumed by an obsessively Anglophobic William Carlos Williams. In the sixties Williams was regarded as the patron saint of the Raw School, whose adherents took on board his literary nationalism and its complex of myths – that Whitman is the poet favoured by the common man, for example, or that free verse is a kind of magic spell which liberates the oppressed (something of this latter notion survives in Language poetry – the belief that writing a poem entirely composed from punctuation marks will help bring down the arms trade). Jarman and Mason quote a 1986 attack on the New Formalists by Diane Wakowski in which she warns of a plot to undermine 'the free verse revolution and the poetry which is the fulfilment of the Whitman heritage' (Dr Williams' rage against Eliot's 'betrayal', one recalls, was couched in similar terms). And she denounces John Hollander as 'Satan'. Is this the meaning of Jarman and Mason's crimson cover? Perhaps the New Formalists need to present themselves as Satanic, as worthy of a fatwah, in order to register as a chapter in literary history.

But when is formalism progressive and when is it reactionary? Few of the poets in this anthology would admit to using form to invoke a spurious historical authority. And many poets considered *avant-garde* have experimented with the restrictions of form. Is there any real difference between Language poet Ron Silliman's strict adherence to a mathematical sequence and Thom Disch's use of the alphabet as a formal device? Perhaps it's all a matter of intention: poem as *utterance* vs. poem as seminar topic. Jarman and Mason probably wouldn't designate Ashbery a New Formalist though he's employed such highly conventional forms as the pantoum and sestina as 'devices for getting into remoter areas of consciousness'. 'The really bizarre requirements of a sestina', he told *New York Quarterly*, 'I use as a probing tool rather than as a form in the traditional sense . . . rather like riding downhill on a bicycle and having the pedals push your feet. I wanted my feet pushed into places they wouldn't normally have taken'. But surely this is *precisely* the function of 'form in the traditional sense' – that serendipity provided by negotiation with a resistant medium, the intervention of what we used to call the muse. Compare Ashbery's strict adherence to the poetry handbook with the methods of those Old Formalists of the fifties (then called the New Formalists. I said this got convoluted) who rarely succumbed to this kind of foot fetish. 'Though I commonly work in meters', wrote Richard Wilbur, 'my way of going about a poem is very like the free verse writer's: that is, I begin by letting the words find what line lengths seem right to them . . . All of my poems, therefore, are formally ad hoc; quite a few are, so far as I know, without formal precedent, and none sets out to fulfil the rules of some standard form'. Perhaps the old New Formalists were of the Devil's party without knowing it, as Blake said of Milton. To confuse matters further, *Rebel Angels* contains many poems in experimental or 'procedural' forms: we find Dana Gioia adapting a fugue form used by Weldon Kees, for example, Thom Disch exhausting the permutations of a rhyme scheme, and

Marilyn Hacker forging a minimalist verse form out of a line from
The Snow Queen.

Apart from these poets already familiar to British readers, *Rebel
Angels* offers all too brief a glimpse of Marilyn Nelson, Charles
Martin, R. S. Gwynn, Greg Williamson, and Rachel Wetzsteon. I
was delighted to discover Molly Peacock, whose giddily enjambed
rhymes drive her erotic poems like a dynamo – commendably erotic
in that Ms Peacock doesn't want to display or exploit desire, she
wants to *understand* it, and rhyme is her vehicle. Mary Jo Salter dis-
plays a similar command of technique. In 'Welcome to Hiroshima'
she writes of wandering that city's Peace Park, dismayed by the
kitsch, until she stops before a display of a sliver of glass:

> . . . a shard the bomb slammed
> in a woman's arm at eight-fifteen, but some
> three decades on – as if to make it plain
> hope's only renewable as pain,
> and as if all the unsung
> debasements of the past may one day come
> rising to the surface once again –
> worked its filthy way out like a tongue.

Rhyme imitates the symmetry of logic, and here Salter exploits this
to reinforce her rhetoric in a technique analogous to a musical
cadence. She interrupts the sentence and the concrete image it con-
veys to shift to an abstract register – future and past, hope and guilt
– like a suspension bridge across the stanza break before resolving
on a single obscenely visceral simile.

Despite their explanations, the editor's selection policy eludes
me. Where, for example, is Gjertrud Schnackenberg? Brooks
Haxton? Vikram Seth? Tim Steele is here, but not his excellent
'Sapphics Against Anger'; the blank verse narratives of Andrew
Hudgins and Sydney Lea take up so many pages one wishes for a
separate anthology of 'New Narrative' poetry; and – this is dis-
turbingly familiar – poets born before 1940 are excluded by fiat.
What's more, there's enough forced rhyme and inert metrically
woozy rhythm in this anthology to suggest that the American ear

has atrophied. Elizabeth Alexander reads like Marilyn Hacker rhyming in her sleep; Bruce Bawer takes most of a sonnet to look out of a plane window and compare the lights below to stars – something that must have occurred to anyone who's ever flown; one could easily imagine Phyllis Levin swapping personifications with Abraham Cowley: 'On the border of the future / Broods the infinite / There knowledge slowly sips her win / And savors it'. I hasten to add that Levin redeems herself with 'The Lost Bee' but hers is a grey lonesome world: 'It was my love upon the bed / who pointed out my silhouette / Anonymous and monochrome'. All too often in *Rebel Angels* that tone of world-weary sophistication intrudes like a sepia pall, as though the climb up Parnassus were too exhausting and the view from the summit a disappointment. Compare this to the new poets writing over here whose use of form signals an increase of energy and momentum.

Rebel Angels contains many surprises and is worth having on your bookshelf. If the ground has shifted during this past decade and American poetry has become more formal across the board, the movement was a success and their anthology can lay it to rest. Rebels or not, the best of these poets deserve better than to be bundled in a pigeonhole.

Dana Gioia

CRITICISM AND HEDONISM

Can Poetry Matter? Essays on Poetry and American Culture
Graywolf Press

'. . . can it be that pleasure makes us objective?'

Roland Barthes, *Pleasures of the Text*

A writer's ideal audience is necessarily imagined, though some writer's audiences are more imaginary than other's. Dana Gioia, exponent of America's New Formalism, lately imagined and coveted a vast sophisticated readership of the literary novel, a readership who long ago regretfully gave up on reading contemporary poetry, but a readership for whom 'formal and narrative verse did not violate any preordained theoretical taboos', who 'unselfconsciously enjoyed rhyme, meter, and storytelling as natural elements of the popular arts like rock, musical theatre, and motion pictures'.

In *Can Poetry Matter? Essays on Poetry and American Culture*, a collection of about twenty-four essays and reviews, he continues to address this intellectual hedonist – and anyone else who cares to listen – with a familiar confidence. An academic would call both Gioia and his reader dilettantes. Both the style of these essays and the message repeated throughout arise from a comfortable faith in this consanguinity. It's a style that has earned him the spluttering rage of many an academic poet. Take the title essay (printed in *PR* 81/4). Demonstrating that the proliferation of poetry in America is proportional to a decline in its readership, Gioia cites, among other causes, the institutional Creative Writing programme. It's one thing to say the emperor is naked, quite another to list the address of his tailor.

> With an average of ten poetry students in each graduate section, these programs alone will produce about 20,000 accredited professional poets over the next decade.

Many of Gioia's angriest critics earn a crust in this system. Wounded, falling back on a cranky equation of free verse with liberation, formalism with regimentation, they have repeatedly characterized him as a reactionary. In a 1988 issue of the *Northwest Review*, in an article entitled 'Dana Gioia And the Poetry of Money', Greg Kuzma attacked him as de facto fascist because at the time he made a living as a corporate businessman. Ariel Dawson, in an article entitled 'The Yuppie Poet' in the *Associated Writing Programs Newsletter*, equated the reemergence of form with Reaganomics and the 'renewed interest in country clubs'. There have been enough of these responses to create an unmanageable backlog at pseud's corner.

His critics in Britain will be disappointed to find he has produced a volume of liberal, infuriatingly *reasonable* criticism. Here are insightful and informative essays on neglected or out-of-fashion poets such as Robinson Jeffers, Ted Kooser, Howard Moss, and the near-mythical Weldon Kees. There's also a marvellous dissection of the phenomenon of Robert Bly ('simplistic, monotonous, insensitive to sound, enslaved by poetic diction, and pompously sentimental'). Bly, most notorious over here as the author of *Iron John* and the risible 'wild man' movement it inspired, has long been an enormously influential figure in American poetry, perhaps the single most influential figure of the sixties and seventies. It is Bly we have to thank for the entire solemn genre of 'Deep Image' prairie surrealism with its slack rhythms, flat diction and cryptic bardic whisper:

> There is a restless gloom in my mind.
> I walk grieving. The leaves are down.
> I come at dusk
> Where, sheltered by poplars, a low pond lies.
> The sun abandons the sky, speaking through cold leaves.

– a passage Gioia renders in a kind of L=A=N=G=U=A=G=E version: 'Restless gloom grieving leaves down dusk low abandons cold.'

He has a genius for the exquisitely wrought barb: when he says that ideas in Ashbery, for example, are 'like the melodies in some jazz improvisation where the musicians have left out the original tune to avoid paying royalties' or when he relineates 'The Red Wheelbarrow' to reveal it as two lines of modulated blank verse masquerading as an eight-line Japanese epiphany. But these are always tempered by an infectious gratitude for the poet's best work.

Somewhat less successful, I think, is his appreciation of Elizabeth Bishop. Here the focus is not so much Bishop and her poetry as the effect of her personal example on Gioia and his circle. Her 'reclusiveness and modesty' are contrasted with Ginsberg's showmanship – 'jangling his finger cymbals like a Hollywood gypsy'. A curious offering, 'Business and Poetry' feels cluttered by unnecessary cataloguing and repetition. Do we need to know the names and careers of so many moonlighting executives? They were undoubtedly included for this book's ideal reader, whose name, its author concedes, is probably Dana Gioia.

Can Poetry Matter? includes only two apologia for the movement, 'Notes on The New Formalism' and 'The Poet In An Age of Prose', and in both essays he applauds the achievements of modernism. As critical readers we should always be wary of the term 'disinterested'. It implies the New Critics and the hidden agenda behind their canon. But as working poets we should welcome Gioia's practicality and aversion to dogma. He could be detailing his own poetic programme when he says that Donald Justice

> assimiliated the achievements of international modernism . . .
> [and] confronted the burden of the past by exploring and con-
> solidating the enduring techniques of modernism to create a style

that reconciled the experiments of the previous two generations with the demands of the present.

In the same essay he calls the intertextual collage of *The Cantos* and *The Waste Land* 'decorative devices, arresting local effects to add interest to the surface of the poem'. This is the aerial perspective. From this height modernism is just a feature of the traditional landscape.

As regards technique, a critic has called me one of the 'New Formalists', and I will accept the label provided it be understood that to try to revive the force of rhyme and other formal devices, by reconciling them with the experimental gains of the past several decades, is itself sufficiently experimental.

Gioia? No, that was Richard Wilbur in 1955, the heyday of disinterested criticism. As early as 1948 Wilbur acknowledged modernism as 'a revolution against trivial formalism, dead rhetoric, and genteel subject matter' whilst announcing a new traditionalist poetic. Like Wilbur and the other formalist poets of the fifties, Gioia is a pragmatist and pluralist, suspicious of ideology. He speaks of 'tradition' not in the magisterial sense in which Eliot wielded the term but of an '*available* tradition . . . namely that small portion of the past a poet finds usable at a particular moment in history'. The keywords here, I think, are 'portion' and 'usable', the language of an enthusiastic technician rattling open a drawer of instruments. In so many words, both poets characterize modernism as a *technical* revolution, whose methods can be assimilated into the (available) tradition.

So what's 'new' about this formalism? Gioia is very keen to distinguish between his contemporaries and the fifties generation of formalists. Both groups 'endorse rhyme and meter as legitimate and "organic" modes of literary composition'. But where Wilbur, Hecht, and Bogan were undeniably elitist and considered themselves guardians of America's European cultural heritage, Gioia and his circle seek to break with the universities and actively engage a general readership using whatever comes to hand.

In this regard *Can Poetry Matter?* differs fundamentally from academic criticism. The issue is pleasure. It is the nature of the scholar to loathe vulgar entertainment. Its pleasures are irrational. The satisfactions of the text are properly analytical. 'Let the crowd swoon at the cinema', says the academic, 'but leave poetry for us.' Consider professors Marjorie Perloff or Jerome McGann who champion the latest 'asyntactical' verbiage precisely *because* 'It does not propose for its immediate object pleasure'.

Berryman said of Randall Jarrell's criticism that he wrote 'always like a human being talking to someone – differing in this from about nine-tenths of what other working American critics manufacture'. Dana Gioia writes in just such a spirit, a spirit genial enough to engage the general reader. The assumptions he shares with this community are liberal. The taste he shares runs to accessibility, discursiveness, and worst of all, *delight* in poetry – a decadent bourgeois down to his chalk-stripe turn ups.

John Keats

A FINE EXCESS

Keats wrote to his friend John Taylor, 'I think Poetry should surprise by a fine excess and not by Singularity . . . and appear almost a Remembrance . . .' Reading this passage again I'm struck by the word 'remembrance'. On a merely technical level, of course, all poetry aspires to the condition of remembrance since all poetry has a common ancestor in song. Poetry isn't just the oldest form of literature – it precedes literature. Imagine a society before the invention of writing: the *only* way of preserving important information. Methods of hunting and navigation, the history of the tribe and its place in the cosmos all have to be cast into a rhythmic pattern and rendered memorizable. In fact, all the 'techniques' we associate today with the art of verse – rhythm, rhyme, simile, striking imagery – are the stock in trade of the vaudeville memory artist. You might say that the techniques we associate with poetry constitute a 'remembering machine'.

But with the invention of print and the rise of literacy poetry became obsolete from a utiliarian standpoint. You don't have to memorize what you can look up. So why has this art form survived in an age of books and films and the Internet? Perhaps something about the nature of verse, the music, the physical texture of words and their effect on the senses communicates on a level prose can't touch, a level of consciousness older than writing.

You can see some of the practical didactic quality of oral poetry in Homer. In the quarrel between Achilles and Agamemnon at the beginning of the *Iliad* he lays out the rules for the disposition of captives, the etiquette of making and receiving ransom requests, the reverence due to priests, etc . . . even instructions on how to launch and land a ship. In Book 23 there's a passage in which the wise old Nestor advises his young son on how to win a chariot race despite having a slower team of horses. (His advice: Hug the post.) Probably saved a few lives.

Once a poem helped save my life. I was living in a basement flat in Chicago one winter at the end of the seventies and I was mired in a terrible depression. I'd given up hope. It was as though someone or something had pulled a plug and the meaning had drained out of everything. The world was still visible out the window, but it was devoid of purpose. Then one night I met a woman in a bar who recited Keats's 'Ode to Melancholy' from memory. And my astonishment at the beauty and terror of the poem seemed to jolt me out of myself. At the risk of sounding like a vicar from the Church of Poetry on 'Thought for the Day', I'd go so far as to say it saved my soul.

In the poem Keats distinguishes between what we moderns call 'Depression' and a passionate sadness he calls 'the Melancholy', not an abstraction, but a goddess he assumes the reader is hunting. It begins *in medias res*. He seems to be already halfway through warning his audience not to seek her in dull numb anguish: 'No, no! go not to Lethe, neither twist / Wolf's-bane, tight-rooted, for its poisonous wine / Nor suffer thy pale forehead to be kist / By nightshade, ruby grape of Prosperpine'.

Keats wrote this poem during that amazing fever of activity between January and September of 1819 when he wrote virtually all his major poetry (like Syvia Plath's final frenzied winter when she wrote her most searing poems). He must have known he didn't have time. He must have known that he was about to succumb to the TB that had just claimed his brother. He was to die in two years, aged twenty-five.

Another aspect of lyric poetry is the way a long-dead poet will insist on his or her continuing presence through the poem. One way a poet creates the illusion of dramatic moment is to hold out his hand and show you something – an inanimate object, like Yorick's skull, a magician's prop towards which he directs our attention so that the magic can take place by sleight of hand. In Keats' 1816 poem to Fanny Brawne there's no object in his hand. It's the hand itself he's showing us, reaching out through the page and across a hundred and eighty-five years.

> This living hand, now warm and capable
> Of earnest grasping, would, if it were cold
> And in the icy silence of the tomb,
> So haunt thy days and chill thy dreaming nights
> That thou wouldst wish thine own heart dry of blood
> So in my veins red life might stream again,
> And thou be conscience-calmed – see here it is –
> I hold it towards you.
> (1816)

On the one level, of course, the poem is just Keats emotionally blackmailing the object of his desire. But it's become something more. Jonathan Culler says of this poem that we fulfil the prophecy by forgetting our own empirical lives and by trying to embrace a fictional time in which the hand 'is really present and perpetually held towards us through the poem.' He says that 'the poem predicts this mystification, dares us to resist it, and shows that its power is irresistible.' I would add that this 'mystification' is simply an extreme and provocative version of the reader's position in reading any poem; the resurrection of the poet's voice depends on the reader's suspension of empirical time as he or she realizes its metre.

This poem's extraordinary ending, in which the most immediate gestural challenge coincides with the closure that contains the poem, poses the problem of what the aesthetic object wants of us. In any act of reading, the reader attempts to restore the words to a source, a human situation involving speech, character, personality. We read a poem to verify the axiom of presence: we read to meet the other.

Ezra Pound

'MY METRO EMOTION'

In the entire shameful history of academic over-interpretation there is no greater disproportion of text to commentary than the case of Pound's little poem about faces on the Paris underground.

It appeared in the 1913 issue of *Poetry*. In 1916 Pound wrote in his memoir on Gaudier-Brzeska that three years previously he'd got out of a 'metro' train at La Concorde, and saw a succession of beautiful faces 'and I tried all that day to find words for what this had meant to me, and I could not find any words that seemed to me worthy, or as lovely as that sudden emotion.'

He goes on to say that he could find no words but in some language of colour; 'little splotches of colour', which is where the petals come in. He then waxes lyrical about Japanese poetry, and he relays a marvellous anecdote given to him by Victor Plarr: 'that once, when Plarr was walking over snow with a Japanese naval officer, they came to a place where a cat had crossed the path, and the officer said, 'Stop, I am making a poem.' Which poem was, roughly, as follows:

> The footsteps of the cat upon the snow:
> (are like) plum-blossoms.'

The words 'are like' would not occur in the original, but I add them for clarity.'

He then gives us a story of the poem's composition which calls to mind Coleridge's story of his composition of 'Xanadu': neither story is completely believable. You have to suspect that both Pound and

Coleridge had a fragment (or in Pound's case a single image) and fabricated a story to make it more interesting. Pound says he 'wrote a thirty-line poem, and destroyed it because it was what we call work "of second intensity".' (Rather conveniently, so we'll have to take his word that he wrote it.) 'Six months later', he says, 'I made a poem half that length; a year later I made the following hokku-like sentence: –

> "The apparition of these faces in the crowd:
> Petals, on a wet, black bough."'

Now obviously the whole trick of the poem is that the colon substitutes for the two words 'is like' and, of course, there's that word 'apparition' which carries a resonance of something spiritual. The critics have gone mad with this. But the chief offender has to be Hugh Kenner in *The Pound Era*:

'We need the title so that we can savor that vegetal contrast with the world of machines: this is not any crowd, moreover, but a crowd seen underground, as Odysseus and Orpheus and Kore saw crowds in Hades.'

So any mention of the underground perforce invokes this classical allusion. Pound himself makes no mention of this in his account of the writing of the poem – for him it's all a matter of 'painting', of getting a visual equivalent for his emotion.

'And carrying forward the suggestion of wraiths'

which hasn't indeed been made

'the word "apparition" detaches these faces from all the crowded faces, and presides over the image that conveys the quality of their separation: *Petals on a wet, black bough.* Flowers, underground; flowers, out of the sun; flowers seen as if against a natural gleam, the bough's wetness gleaming on its darkness, in this place where wheels turn and nothing grows. The mind is touched, it may be, with a memory of Persephone, as we read of her in the 106th Canto *Dis'bride, Queen over Phlegethon, girls faint as mist about her.* The faces of those girls likewise "apparitions".'

So it's Demeter and Persephone just because faces in a station look like petals? This critical hairiness calls for Occam's razor.

'It is a simile with "like" suppressed:'

Right! Now, no doubt, he'll tell us this was never done before!

'So this tiny poem, drawing on Gauguin and on Japan, on ghosts and on Persephone, on the Underworld and on the Underground, the Metro of Mallarme's capital and a phrase that names a station of the Metro as it might a station of the Cross,'

Christ! Now he's dragged the Crucifixion into it!

'concentrates far more than it need ever specify, and indicates the means of delivering post-Symbolist poetry from its pictorialist impasse . . . The mind that found 'petals on a wet, black bough' had been active (and for more than a year on that poem, off and on).'

So we are told.

'The "plot" of the poem is that mind's activity, fetching some new thing into the field of consciousness.'

So now this two-line poem has a plot! And the plot is that the poet thought of it!

Elizabeth Bishop

THE EXILE'S ACCENT

Ever play that parlour game where you answer one snatch of song with another? Listen:

> As I walked out one evening
> Walking down Bristol Street
> The crowds upon the pavement
> Were fields of harvest wheat.

> > – Wheat, not oats, dear. I'm afraid
> > if it's wheat it's none of your sowing,
> > nevertheless I'd like to know
> > what you are doing and where you are going.

Two stanzas by – you might say – two very different poets. But this trick works because Auden and Bishop share a tone – that 'dear' could have easily come from Auden. We normally associate Bishop with Lowell and Marianne Moore, and we know she had sections of Stevens' *Harmonium* by heart and we can readily see these influences in her work – but they don't account for that arch, intimate tone, that formal flourish. Bonnie Costello has suggested Bishop learned more from Auden than any of her contemporaries.

In 1974, Bishop wrote 'A Brief Reminiscence and a Brief Tribute' on Auden for the *Harvard Advocate*. She concludes:

These verses and many, many more of Auden's have been part of my mind for years – I could say, part of my life . . . When I was in college, and all through the thirties and forties, I and all my friends who were interested in poetry read him constantly. We hurried to see his latest poem or book, and either wrote as much like him as possible, or tried hard not to . . . We admired his apparent toughness, his sexual courage – actually more honest than Ginsberg's, say, is now, while still giving expression to technically dazzling poetry. Even the most hermetic early poems gave us the feeling there here was someone who knew – about psychology, geology, birds, love, the evils of capitalism – what have you? They colored our air and made us feel tough, ready, and in the know, too.

Bishop plays a similarly pivotal role in my development as a writer. As a young poet sending my work about, I'd get 'encouraging' rejections from American magazine editors who found my work promising but 'affected', who felt I hadn't 'found my natural voice'. This was the seventies, and the contents page of most school anthologies of twentieth-century American poetry started (and in a sense ended) with William Carlos Williams. They tended to document the 'natural' and 'confessional' and downplay or reject the influence of Auden – that arch elegance, that courageous affectation – a tone I recognized in the work of two of the poets I most revered: James Merrill and Elizabeth Bishop – a somewhat campy note of displacement resolved by conspicuous technique, a mode defined by wit – in the Renaissance sense – irony, seduction, and playfulness alloyed with reserve. I've heard it said that artists often emigrate as a strategy to disguise a chronic private exile. I thought of all those poets whose craft is driven not by a desire to express a confidently anchored 'natural' self, but by a need to create a self through the work. Bishop provided a model.

Bishop's poetic 'accent' was forged by a very real exile. In 'A Country Mouse' she tells of her childhood rejection of American identity after she'd been taken from her grandparents' home in Canada. (Contrast this with William Carlos Williams's childhood experience and subsequent literary nationalism.) Perhaps this crisis helped her escape the two-party system of American poetry. It's hard to steer your own course when the river keeps channelling into

Whitman's yawp or Dickinson's centripedal concision, especially if you're seeking a current that's 'dark, salt, clear, moving, and utterly free'. And maybe it helped her access more freely the tradition of English poetry.

Costello has discovered in the Vassar library Bishop's unfinished 1937 review of Auden's *Look, Stranger!* which she calls 'The Mechanics of Pretense: Remarks on W.H. Auden'. Pretence, she argues, is a way of bringing something into being (children pretend to speak a foreign language and grow up linguists; small nations pretend grandeur and become empires). So a poet facing a different world from that of his forebears pretends the existence of a language to match a reality or feeling that is not yet articulate. Bishop writes:

> In his earlier stages the poet is the verbal actor. One of the causes of poetry must be, we suppose, the feeling that the contemporary language is not equivalent to the contemporary fact; there is something out of proportion between them, and what is being said in words is not at all what is being said in 'things'. To correct this disproportion a pretence is at first necessary. By 'pretending' the existence of a language appropriate and comparable to 'things' it must deal with, the language is forced into being. It is learned by one person, by a few, by all who can become interested in that poet's poetry.

Pretence is a mechanism by which a self is invented for every poem, either a persona like Robinson Crusoe, or a housemaid, or the Riverman, or 'an Elizabeth' who inhabits us for the duration of the poem. American poetry at the end of this century seems less rigidly 'fundamentalist' and more open to true poetic decorum, that continuous negotiation between subject and style. Looking back, though, I'm grateful to all those hostile editors and critics who, appalled by my propensity for rhyme and metre, rejected my poems and gave me time to develop my own range of 'unnatural' voices.

I'd like to conclude by looking at one of Bishop's most admired lyrics, 'The Shampoo'. She wrote this in 1952 – first included in a letter to Marianne Moore, but it made the rounds of umpteen

magazines including the *New Yorker* and *Poetry* before it was
finally published in the *New Republic* in 1955. A true metaphysical
love lyric, its conceit – a contrast between human and natural time
scales – built like a ribcage about its emotional core.

> The still explosions on the rocks,
> the lichens, grow
> by spreading, gray, concentric shocks.
> They have arranged
> to meet the rings around the moon, although
> within our memories they have not changed.

On the one hand time's cyclical, immeasurably slow as the grey con-
centric shocks of lichen on the boulders which have – listen for the
social nuance here – arranged to meet the rings around the moon.
On the other hand it can be linear. In the second stanza Bishop
addresses her dear friend (Lota, of course):

> And since the heavens will attend
> as long on us,
> you've been, dear friend,
> precipitate and pragmatical;
> and look what happens. For Time is
> nothing if not amenable.

Precipitate and pragmatical – an odd pairing of adjectives. Surely,
we say, she means to oppose these qualities: rash but practical. But,
as she told her writing class at Harvard: 'Always use the dictionary;
it's better than the critics.' If precipitate connotes rash, the obsolete
pragmatical can mean meddlesome. So this is a gentle rebuke: 'And
look what happens' – time 'nothing if not amenable' appears to
comply with this attitude and hasten its pace. And what form does
it take as it streaks through space? The shooting stars in your
black hair which recalls precipitate and the suggestion of a chemical
precipitate falling out of its solution to rest at the bottom of a glass.

> The shooting stars in your black hair
> in bright formation

are flocking where,
so straight, so soon?
– Come, let me wash it in this big tin basin,
battered and shiny like the moon.

What goes without saying? The bleak answer to where those stars
are flocking? The tenderness and simplicity of the gesture in the
last two lines? Or the way Bishop invites her beloved to step outside
of time with her and meet the rings around their own battered and
shiny artificial moon?

MISCELLANEOUS PIECES

My Report Card

(2000)

1. '. . . a fidgety affectation of style after style which suggests that unlike more mature poets of his generation, Donaghy has not yet found his voice'. F. Olsen, 'Noted in Brief', *Hierophant*, Spring 1993.

2. Thales teaches that all things are full of gods. Anaximenes teaches that every stone on the beach has a soul. I'd certainly credit a page of poetry with a mind of its own. In our desire to locate the presence of the poet behind the frame of the words, we tend to animate the poem – the organic analogy – so it seems to be *returning* our attention, or we breathe life into its inanimate imagery – a marble torso of Apollo, London's mighty heart, a wafer lifted and consecrated.

3. Proust recalls his mother at Combray, how gracefully she'd turn a social blunder to her advantage 'like good poets whom the tyranny of rhyme forces into the discovery of their finest lines'. I'm in it for the discovery. If writing poems were merely a matter of bulldozing ahead with what you'd already made up your mind to say I'd have long ago given it up for something more dignified.

4. Must get round to reading 'The Feeling of a Presence and Verbal Meaningfulness in Context of Temporal Lobe Function: Factor Analytic Verification of the Muses?', Persinger, Michael A.; Makarec, Katherine, *Brain and Cognition*, 1992, November, Vol. 20 (2): 217–26. Persinger and Makarec (to quote from the abstract) hypothesize that the profound sensation of a presence, particularly during periods of profound verbal creativity in reading or writing prose or poetry, is an endemic cognitive phenomenon. Factor analyses of twelve clusters of phenomenological experiences from

348 men and 520 women (aged 18–65 years), who enrolled in undergraduate psychology courses over a ten-year period, supported the hypothesis. The authors conclude that periods of intense meaningfulness (a likely correlate of enhanced burst-firing in the left hippocampal-amygdaloid complex and temporal lobe) allow access to nonverbal representations that are the right hemispheric equivalents of the sense of self; they are perceived as a presence.

5. One morning in the sixties when I was queuing outside the confessional in church it impressed my adolescent soul that the adults milling about me were guilty of an original sin of arrogance, of assuming it was they and not the massed total of their experience that had sinned. One way to cope with such moments of vertigo is to experiment with different signatures, other voices. (See under 'poetry' and 'confessional', separate entries.)

6. Must look into forming some kind of movement and drafting a manifesto. Also, must try to be more direct. *Poetry's a way of thinking; a clarity between the truth of music and the truth.* See? No sooner are the words out but they turn to lead. It's embarrassing to talk about one's own poetry in prose, which may be why we have to endure so many poems about poetry.

7. Whenever I get the urge to write a poem about poetry I take a cold shower.

8. Which reminds me, MANIFESTOS ARE RIDICULOUS. Key scene: the mountainous silhouette of Charles Foster Kane emerging from behind the editor's desk waving his 'Declaration of Principles', and Jedidiah requesting the draft for a souvenir: 'I have a feeling it's going to be worth something one day,' he grins, 'like my first report card.'

9. 'the horror of the forest, or the silent thunder afloat in the leaves, not the intricate dense wood of the trees' (Mallarmé); 'a wind with a smell of children's spittle, crushed grass, and a jellyfish veil which announces the constant baptism of newly created things' (Lorca).

10. Must try harder at sport.

A Backward Glance

Most British poets I've met feel they must come to terms with American poetry. The Americans have their own way of coming to terms with British poetry: they ignore it. I've just returned from a series of readings in New York and Chicago where I was repeatedly introduced as representing a distinctly British or Irish 'style'. There was much said about tradition and experimentation, Larkin and Pound. I won't bore you. Then I'd get up and read poems rejected by one British publisher because they were 'distinctly American'.

Well, maybe he was right. I certainly read a lot of American verse when I lived there. But the handful of living poets I most admired were not American, and nowadays there are so many competing strains of influence and allegiance on the American scene it would take a Linnaeus to classify them all. Chatting with my hosts after these events I got the impression that 'American poet' has become a blanket term for several wildly different kinds of artist.

Many are professional creatures, products of one of the more than two hundred and fifty creative writing programs offering advanced degrees and impossibly pretentious credentials. (One can be a Doctor of Poetry in America these days.) Seduced and abandoned by academic literary criticism, it seems the poets have gone and founded their own academies. Former countercultural firebrand Allen Ginsberg, for example, is now Professor Emeritus Ginsberg at his very own academy-in-the-clouds, the Naropa Institute. And there are so many gurus to choose from: Greg Kuzma claims that 'Within five years there will be a creative-writing program available for anyone in America within safe driving distance of his home'. A typical assignment in these classes, I'm told, is a poem a week – whether or not one has anything to say – and after graduation one is expected to publish a collection and go on to teach . . . creative writing. This bizarre inbreeding has produced a new kind of academic verse, not the bookish stuff literary critics do for a hobby, but the unique idiom of full-time writer-teachers.

Am I being unfair? I suppose it necessarily must be a good thing to have all those programmes and prizes, all that time and money devoted to poetry. But I'm suspicious. I bet you are too.

In the meantime, the literature departments have struck back and produced their own, less democratic breed of poet. This may be the first time poets have been created as a footnote to the critical apparatus set up to interpret them. Lately two opposing camps have emerged, something like the Big Endians and the Small Endians, but not so political.

On the small end, or cutting edge, we have the L=A=N=G=U=A=G=E poets, who write 'asyntactical' verse – daring experimental arrangements of words which to our untrained eyes look like meaningless drivel. This is because we haven't read the sophisticated post-structuralist essays written by its apologists. We're like those Philistines who didn't appreciate Op Art because they didn't subscribe to *Arts Review*. The typical L=A=N=G=U=A=G=E poem reads like something screeched from the stage of the Cabaret Voltaire in 1919 by a woman in a cardboard hat, so I hope I'm forgiven for noting along with Auden that 'everything changes but the avant garde'.

I didn't get to read any of the opposition but I'm told they represent the old pre-structuralist end of the egg. They are called Expansionists or New Formalists, which, oddly enough, was the name given to another group of poets in the early fifties – Lowell, Wilbur, Merrill and Viereck. Like that earlier rear guard, they've begun by trafficking respectfully in villanelles and sestinas, which is a little like donning a laurel crown and toga and announcing the return of the golden age.

From this little distance the varieties of American poetry might suggest a Lilliputian squabble over style, a purely literary dispute. But they are much more than that. They are varieties of American faith: the Emersonian programme of self-improvement advanced by the writing teachers, that touching faith in progress held by the avant garde who think that literature advances like a kind of technology, and the fundamentalist belief in a stable tradition. If the distinctly American poet ever existed, I'm afraid he's gone the way of the buffalo, the timber wolf and the passenger pigeon.

On being a New Generation Poet

Dear Peter and Kevan,

I've done my best with this. It was pure duty. I trust you to print only what you find interesting.

Questionnaire

1) Three books:
My principal influences aren't 20th century. But, since you ask, there's no escaping that lunatic Yeats (*The Tower*). Paul Muldoon redirected me to Frost, his ear, his palimpsest ironies (*Complete Poems*, 1949). For my third choice, I considered prose (Borges) but Derek Mahon's *The Snow Party* brought me back to poetry when I thought I'd almost given up.

2) Special poetic affinity:
I read and enjoy the work of many of the poets listed among the 'New Generation Poets'. No movements or manifestos, but many of us readily concede the same names among our favourite reading: some of us might express an affinity with Auden, MacNeice and Bishop, some with Frank O'Hara. But you won't catch many of us acknowledging a debt to Charles Olson, say, or J. H. Prynne.

3) Does 'Postmodernism' have any useful meaning?
No more than the term 'water' has any useful meaning for a fish. I notice, however, that I feel distinctly uncomfortable when asked to comment on my own work or say what it's 'about'. I'm told this is a characteristic symptom of the condition. This worries me, as most

literature called postmodern seems to be exclusively concerned with its own production.

4) Positive/Negative:

Didn't care for this question, and I'd prefer you didn't print my response, but this is roughly how I feel about some things on the list:

* 20s Modernism: 1) several exciting talents. 2) a style that ossified into dogma
* Auden and Co.: Very positive, but only if 'Co.' means MacNeice.
* 40s NeoRomantics: never read them.
* The Movement: fail to see how Larkin and Davie can be part of the same movement '. . . even the straightest / Of issues looks pretty oblique / When a movement turns into a clique' (Amis)
* Black Mountain: A suitable case for deprogramming. Olson was a cult leader with all of Pound's crankiness and none of his talent.
* The Beats: See Modernism. For 'dogma' read 'pose'.
* The Martians: died off when exposed to Earth's bacteria.
* The New Poetry: A book containing many good poems. No parodist could improve upon the introduction. A embarrassment of postgraduate swot diction. Or is that postcognitive?
* Sumerian Chic: Does this mean posing with a ziggurat holder?

5) Should talk of movements be discouraged?

Yes. 'Movements' are dreamt up by publicists to help us sell poetry or by journalists and academic bores to help us misunderstand it.

I want to say 'My poems speak for themselves!' I expect we all do. They have their own lives to lead. For those of you who don't know my poems, there's a lot about memory in them. Memory and history and music and sex and drinking. I hope you find them memorable – or at least memorizable.

Recently, a hostile reviewer dismissed them like this:

'His poems are not confessional, but it helps to think of a Confessional – a little box with a screen separating two parties. Think of that screen as the page. A voice seems to come from behind the screen, but if you read the poem aloud the only voice you hear is your own.' (Florence Olsen in *Haymarket*, Autumn, '93).

I can live with that. The kitschy painting reproduced on the front of *Shibboleth* is 'The hand submits to the intellect'. The picture suggests a more equal partnership. It isn't a matter of 'mastering' a form, but negotiating with and frequently surrendering to it so that I discover the poem as I go (the intellect submitting to the hand) rather than just translating prose ideas into verse. 'My poems speak for themselves!' You're on your own from here.

On naming *Conjure*

It's embarrassing to discuss your own poems in print. You either come across as an awestruck fan of your own genius or as a tedious explainer of jokes. Might as well save time and submit your effort directly to pseud's corner. But as the PBS has reminded me of my duty for the third time this week, I'd best make a start.

First off, my apologies for the title of this book. God knows I resisted it – too hieratic, I thought, too romantic, too *dry ice*. And I appreciate the valiant efforts of all those wiser friends who fought on my side, even the one who suggested I call it *Grimoire*. But we lost. In the end these poems insisted on banding together under a word that could easily appear on a perfume bottle or computer game. But let me list a few reasons in *Conjure*'s defence.

First, it's an imperative, a command to perform *magic* – a word which in turn could mean anything along a scale that runs from Jesus to Tommy Cooper. I mean by such blasphemy to suggest that all the trickery of art, the hours spent practising the deception, perfecting the sleight of hand or calculated ineptitude, is a necessary distraction for both the illusionist and the audience so that some genuine transformation can take place in our heads. The ritual gesture wherein I hold the Jack of diamonds up for your scrutiny before changing it into the very card you picked earlier is *hocus pocus*, a corruption of *hoc est corpus*, wherein I elevate a sliver of bread and change nothing of its appearance, though as Aquinas tells us, the species of the Eucharist has been sanctified. The poetry readings I attend are sometimes like in-house performances at the magic circle. An audience of fellow professionals sits back taking notes or wondering where the performer bought his rabbit. My aim in writing these poems, however, was to address both the initiates of poetry's magic circle as well as a broader congregation. And thanks to the PBS I may get to do both.

Secondly, *conjure* derives from Latin *conjurare*, to swear together, suggesting a ritual performed by two or more celebrants, not a solitary act. I tried to avoid talking to myself in the reader's presence because it's rude. But I invite my readers to play the role of eavesdroppers and hope they won't insist on knowing precisely who I'm talking to (even if it's them). I fancy I'm bound by the sanctity of the *confessional* – not as in 'confessional poetry', mind, but the box where the sacrament is conducted. It's pointless to speculate, and I'm not about to say, whether any given poem in this collection is a fable or an indiscreet disclosure slipped in to satisfy some readers' appetite for 'intensity'. The facts of my little life are beside the point. I tried to tell the truth by working truly.

Thirdly, I'm struck by a peculiar connotation this verb once enjoyed in its long history. 'Nay, I'll *conjure* too', says Mercutio, lampooning Romeo's new role as love-sick erotic poet, 'Romeo! humours! madman! passion! lover! / Appear thou in the likeness of a sigh: / Speak but one rhyme, and I am satisfied; / Cry but 'Ay me!' pronounce but 'love' and 'dove;' . . . I *conjure* thee by Rosaline's bright eyes, By her high forehead and her scarlet lip, / By her fine foot, straight leg and quivering thigh / And the demesnes that there adjacent lie, / That in thy likeness thou appear to us! . . . t'would anger him / To raise a spirit in his mistress' circle / Of some strange nature, letting it there stand / Till she had laid it and conjured it down; / That were some spite: my invocation / Is fair and honest, and in his mistress' name / I *conjure* only but to raise up him.' The meaning of *raising a spirit in his mistress' circle* is echoed in an anonymous eighteenth-century song sent me recently by a friend in which a young man can't sleep because he's troubled by a common complaint of youth: 'So vigourously the spirit stood, / Let him do what he can, / Sure then he said it must be laid, / By woman not by man.' A handsome maid is enlisted who 'having such a guardian care, / her office to discharge; / She opened wide her conjuring book, / And laid the leaves at large.' Little in these poems is designed to conjure such frisky spirits up or down, but I confess I've returned to the ms. again and again over the past seven years, often in the dead of night, with an obsession comparable only to my more goatish impulses. Nevertheless, I hope *conjure* lives up to its Latin origins, *a ritual performed by two or more celebrants*, not the solitary act.

Finally it's *Conjure* because it's dedicated to a master conjurer whose assistance in writing these poems has been invaluable. He was only four last April, but I hope someday he'll be able to read this apology for writing him such a gloomy, rainy, and sometimes brutal book. And I hope he'll read these thanks, too, for forcing me to improvise so many fables when we were both half asleep, and recalling me, whenever necessary, to that world where, in the hour it took to write this report, two blue Lego blocks have conversed gently and consoled each other with kisses before barking and flying away.

Nightwaves: notes for radio broadcast

Any poet's ideal reader is always a ghostly composite. Unlike the writer of a love letter or a telegram who has in his mind's eye the face of the very particular recipient, the poet addresses a composite of

a) all the poet's contemporaries in poetry

b) all his deceased influences in poetry

c) all his friends and family, and lastly, of course **himself**.

By the same token, *readers* must realize that the poet, too, is a ghostly compound of fact and invention.

The new book may seem to be more autobiographical but that's only partly the case.

There's a powerful gossipy cachet invoked when a poet appears to be revealing some intense real-life secret. It's only natural. But I've always resisted this – not because I'm an especially reticent or private individual – but because I really believe a poem has a life of its own and is as much 'about' the reader's life as about mine.

It's the emotional and musical truth, rather than the documentary truth I'm after. I'm not sure I'm a reliable narrator of events even to myself. So a story told from the point of view of a Japanese courtesan or an early Christian saint may be as or more autobiographical than a poem about my father rigging up a doorbell under the table so he could get off the phone without giving offence.

What sets the 'confessional poets' Snodgrass, Lowell, Sexton and Plath apart from other poets who incorporate details from life is their sense of self-revelation and their artful simulation of sincerity. By relying on the documentary truth, on 'real' situations and relationships, for a poem's emotional authenticity, the poet makes an artifice of honesty. Confessional poems, in other words, lie like truth.

All Poets Are Mad

Plato warned that poets are powerless to indite a verse or chant an oracle until they are put out of their senses so that their minds are no longer in them, and ever since no one feels entirely comfortable sharing a cab with one. In fact, a cabbie once pulled over and ordered me out when my travelling companion introduced me as a poet. Incredible? Mind you, my friend had just introduced himself as 'a philosopher'. Normal people don't want to hear that sort of thing. But I'm sure it wasn't always as humiliating as it has been in these days of professionalism, promotion and 'bringing poetry to the people', running after them imploring, *Come back! It doesn't have to rhyme!* The moderns were dignified, right? Apart from Edith Sitwell's turban, I mean. Tell me Yeats got a bit of diced swede stuck in his ear dodging a food fight on an Arvon Schools course. Tell me Pound saw his photo in the local *Advertiser* under the headline RHYMESTER EZ SEZ POETRY IS EASY AND FUN. Up until the end of the war Pound thought humiliation meant having to work in a bank. I guess public readings have changed everything.

Take the case of Dylan Thomas. But there's a class / gender issue there. Sure, many (most?) poets take a drink, often to legendary excess. But name me three working-class male poets not already in AA who don't routinely douse their brains out after every reading. And oh, afterwards! The waking up still drunk next to a strange woman, waking up next to a man, or an animal! Waking up beside a strange dead male animal in a pool of . . . well, in a pool. And *teaching* poetry! Coaching your students in the finer points of rhetoric and prosody so they too can experience the misspelled rejection slips, the personally inscribed copies of their books in the charity shops, the reading fee consisting of the festival souvenir mug and book token, the laid-on meal at McDonald's, the floor spots who make up half the audience and who all leave before – no – during your first poem, and the MC who introduces you as Matthew Sweeney. Twice. And best of all, the waking up alone in the middle of the night biting and tearing at the sweaty hotel sheets whimpering no no no.

Am I confusing the humiliations visited upon poets with the humiliations poets create for themselves? The business already provides plenty without any help from me so I no longer mix drink and verse. Not much. But I used to put away a bottle of vodka during my readings. It wasn't nerves. It was shame. I'd secretly fill the regulation pitcher by the lectern and appear to be knocking back water after every poem. As you do. But drink only ever made things worse. Once after reading at the Poetry Society I saw a pattern of pages laid out on the bookshop floor where a member of staff had been painstakingly collating his concrete poem consisting of large bar codes. I'm told I blurted something about *hopscotch*, broke free of the friends who were carrying me to the door, and executed what was later described as 'an ape dance' all over his efforts.* I remember the shock turning to rage on his face as I slowly realized what I'd done. He would *not* forgive me, though I hung from his lapels weeping, pleading with him to accept my apology. I had subjected myself to another indignity. As for the concrete poet, I was the indignity poetry had inflicted upon him. In *Keats and Embarrassment*, a book I was once caught out pretending to have read, Christopher Ricks suggests that indignation drives out embarrassment, *one hot flush*

---

* Years later I turned a corner in a friend's house and accidentally stepped on a newly completed stained-glass window which had been laid on the floor for a moment just prior to installation. It had taken a year to make. Why am I telling you this?

drives out the other, as fire fire. And speaking of driving, a generous arts officer once gave me a lift back to the station the morning after a reading and for her kindness watched me sicken, open her car door, miss the tarmac and fill the map pocket, drowning her *Leeds A–Z* in an acid indigo porridge of red wine, Jameson's and aubergine curry. Many years passed before I was invited back to Leeds. And once I was sick on Paul Farley. He *forgave* me. People do. That's the worst part, isn't it? Phoning round the next day to grovel and being told, 'No, no, you were *charming*!'

You were charming, darling, because you slotted into a little niche in the cliché centre of the brain. You impish rogue, you. You dangerous firebrand, you. You profound sage, you consumptive aesthete, you holy fool. You silly ponce. *Get out of my cab.*

Introduction to *The May Anthologies 2001*

Last night I dined with a successful art forger. Anonymity being the mark of success in his profession, neither you nor the authorities will have heard of him, but he excels in the manufacture of antique artifacts. The acquisition of technique, he explained, is just a matter of patient attention. The great difficulty, however, is eliminating the contemporaneity of one's taste: unsuccessful forgers tend to incorporate in their productions all the antique characteristics they've studied, and all the modern characteristics of which they remain unaware. Hence, an Etruscan stone goddess forged in 1932 will betray to the modern eye the art deco flair of a flapper.

My criminal friend seemed to be offering me a hard lesson about verse. The very worst poets write principally to assure themselves and their readers that they are indeed poets. To this end they produce forgeries in which they incorporate all they've absorbed from their reconnaissance of contemporary verse – and nothing else. The best of us are quite the opposite of counterfeiters. But in our earnest pursuit of the right word, the unadulterated vision, we're just as capable of cluttering our work with poetic diction and cliché.

In selecting the poems for this anthology. I considered Wordsworth's enumeration of the poetic banalities of his age (in his Preface to *Lyrical Ballads*) and his promise that his readers would find these 'utterly rejected as an ordinary device to elevate the style and raise it above prose'. So I was particularly alert to current clichés like 'deconstructed' syntax, that contemporary equivalent of Victorian inversion, and leaden 'experimental' obscurity. On the positive side, I was looking for clarity, daring, a sense of line, and a willingness to meet the reader halfway. And I found these among a broad spectrum of voices ranging from the onieiric to the satiric, the narrative to the rhetorical. It was my pleasure to hear these new voices and now it's your turn.

Storm the Earth and Stun the Air: Introduction to
101 Poems About Childhood

There's an assumption abroad nowadays that poetry and childhood are naturally linked, that if you write poetry you must perforce also write children's poetry or be charmingly or sadly childlike yourself. And poets are expected to be obsessed with recording the details of their early years, rehearsing their gauzy raptures or picking at the scabs of abuse. I'm sure there are sound, boring reasons for all this involving the economics of publishing and the clichés of journalism, but I think poetry and childhood may be entwined on a deeper level. We first encounter poems in the form of nursery rhymes. We learn much of our language through verse, and, largely due to the resistance and exclusivity of contemporary serious poetry, many adults today only encounter poems as something they read to their kids at bedtime, kids who will soon enter into their own verse culture of rude playground chants, skipping rhymes and taunts and who will, a few years later, learn rock lyrics and rap by heart.

In one sense, all poetry is kids' stuff. What makes us recognize a piece of writing as a poem is often a 'technique' whereby poets imitate children's thinking. Rhyme and rhythm, of course, are the very stuff of the nursery rhymes and dandling songs with which cultures the world over prompt their children toward speech. But even those more sophisticated and 'literary' effects we learn to recognize and name in school have their roots in childhood. When Baudelaire, for example, writes that some perfumes are as sweet as the sound of an oboe or fresh as a child's embrace, we say he's using a technique called *synaesthesia* whereby a sensation in one sense triggers an image or sensation in another. But some psychologists hold that we all experience sensation in this undifferentiated way up to about four months of age. When Rilke tells us that a headless statue looks at us, or Elizabeth Bishop tells us that a knife will not look at her, we say they're employing *personification*, but a substantial school of psychoanalysis traces all such metaphors back to the crib, to that 'special' blanket or teddy bear, the 'transitional object' by which toddlers negotiate separation from their mothers. When Wordsworth describes the earth 'Apparelled in celestial light / The glory and the freshness of a dream', or when Traherne claims to have beheld in his angel infancy the shadows of eternity in clouds and flowers, we know they're not just framing theological arguments, but reporting early experiences of startling clarity. Some neurologists argue that as infants our consciousness is extraordinarily intense and receptive and that during this period we're terribly vulnerable, requiring longer periods of parenting than any other animal. They argue that language delimits that consciousness to manageable chunks, a powerful evolutionary advantage, like an opposable thumb. Only occasionally, they argue, are adults permitted to return to that awestruck state before we framed the world in words. Perhaps poetry is our way of using the power of language against itself so that, however briefly, we see and feel the world afresh, with all the intensity of infancy. What about abstract thought? I hear you ask. After all, we expect wisdom from poets, as we expect it from philosophers and cosmologists. In fact, we expect them all to pose the very same questions children ask: What is *is*? Why is there anything? And why doesn't it all happen at once? Like children's art, children's speculative thought shows a resourcefulness and curiosity missing from most adults.

So you might say every poem invokes childhood on some level. But I had to be somewhat particular in choosing a mere 101 for this anthology. Be advised: this is not a book of children's poetry. Much of it is challenging and some of it bleak. There are dead children here, but it's not a collection of elegies. And while I couldn't resist some ecstatic observations of children by parents and poems of parental love, remorse and responsibility, it's not really a book about parenthood either.

I resisted the impulse to show off by making clever connections through time and decided instead to play the historian, ordering the poems chronologically to illustrate the development of childhood through the ages. Of course, it wound up fairly distorted. There's a gap of about two thousand years between the first and second items, for one thing, and I've included so few poems in translation readers may wonder why I bothered. Childhood, as distinct from children, didn't really exist before the seventeenth century and poets rarely considered children except to mourn their deaths, yet I've given Traherne and Vaughan more than their fair share in order to mark the invention of childhood and the developing idea of childhood spirituality. There are plenty of nineteenth-century poems condemning child labour, but most of them aren't any good. So I let Blake, Browning, and Meynell represent that line. And I've omitted the deluge of mawkish Victoriana, though you can spot shadings of it in Hood and Swinburne. The disproportionate number of twentieth-century poems in these pages reflects the rise of psychoanalysis and the increasing conviction that childhood holds the key to what we are. As Adam Phillips says, with the invention of childhood comes a new kind of person, one with a private inner world. So it's not surprising that the growth in poems about children and childhood parallels the decline of public poetry and the expectation that a poet speaks for and to the public. The poetry of childhood also fills the gap left by the decline of religious poetry. Where poets of previous centuries were principally concerned with where their souls were headed, twentieth-century poets are far more concerned with where they came from. Where Traherne and Vaughan only looked back to their innocence to catch a glimpse of the heaven from whence it issued, modern poets look back to childhood itself as the source of all meaning.

American Revolutions

Let me say at the outset that I'm always honoured to be asked to speak in the Voice Box. Last night I read an essay by the late Eric Mottram in which he described this room as 'the poetry centre for a largely establishment cultural structure' which I find terribly reassuring. And I'm delighted, too, to be asked to speak in this series though I'm perplexed at once again finding myself addressing the subject of American poetry.

Although I was poetry editor of a magazine called the *Chicago Review* during the late seventies and early eighties and just beginning to get my own work published, I was far more interested in the new poetry from Britain and Ireland. I know that must sound bizarre to anyone writing here in the seventies who looked to America for inspiration.

I began writing poems in the Bronx in the sixties, and in the winter of '77 I travelled to the arctic wastes of Chicago to do a PhD in English, because I assumed that's what one did with one's love of literature. Little did I suspect that what had been known as the Neo-Aristotelian, or 'critical pluralist', or 'Chicago school' of criticism was about to be shouldered aside by the Yale school, culminating with the arrival on campus of Derrida himself in '82. If you've read Robert M. Pirsig's *Zen and the Art of Motorcycle Maintenance* and remember his hero's experience of study at the University of Chicago, you have an uncannily close picture of my own experience, breakdown and all.

Gradually I became aware that professing English because I loved poems was like practising vivisection because I loved dogs. One day I mentioned casually to one of my teachers that the 'text' under discussion wasn't to my taste. He looked puzzled. 'But taste is just here,' he said, pointing to his tongue – implying that texts were selected for the canon according to some principle higher than mere quality. I started to spend less time at my carrel in the library and began attending staff meetings of the *Chicago Review*, a magazine which had developed a reputation for publishing controversial material. A few years previously an entire print run containing a piece by William Burroughs had been confiscated by the University. We sued, and won. Not such a smart move, as we were funded by the University. When I found the offices they'd been banished to an unheated basement on the outskirts of campus.

I was astonished to find that my colleagues on the magazine, all graduate students subsidized to be arbiters of literary taste, knew nothing about poetry on this side of the Atlantic. I remember the general editor, now a prominent authority on modernism, asking me – in 1979 – 'Who is this See-amuss Heaney anyway?'

For my co-editors, contemporary poetry was synonymous with the high modernist mode. Not surprising, as modernism appeared to be the only twentieth-century phenomenon they were capable of studying. A few statistics: by 1965, some 2,700 academic books and articles had been devoted to T. S. Eliot. By the late seventies, the estimate had risen to 4,319. The current total exceeds 10,000. By the time I left America, there were at least 5,390 books and articles on Ezra Pound and that's just the English-language contribution. When I left in 1985 I thought I was leaving it all behind.

So it's clear I'm not presenting myself as an unbiased academic or dispassionate literary historian. And you wouldn't believe me if I tried. Maybe we no longer believe in such creatures. We all know that history is written by the victors. A corollary of this is that it's rewritten by the grandchildren of the defeated. To quote Robert Lowell out of context, 'Alas, I can only tell my own story.'

The point of my title is that the seventies brought to the forefront a dialectic which has driven American poetry for two centuries – a war between two tendencies variously decribed as 'raw and cooked', 'palefaces and redskins', 'oppositional and accomodational' and most damaging, I think, 'left and right'. If sometimes it's difficult to tell who's who in the skirmishes of this literary history it's because poets, like Mormons, make a practice of bapitizing pagans into their own Church.

Briefly, it all begins with Emerson. We habitually misread Emerson through Walt Whitman. We preserve and selectively quote an Emerson who is a John the Baptist to Whitman's Jesus. So we often hear quoted Emerson's famous dictum 'It is not metre, but a metre making argument that makes the poem' invoked as the original American free verse manifesto. But Emerson goes on to say that for the new American poet, 'the thought and the form are equal in the order of time, but in the order of genesis the thought is prior to the form' making a strangely medieval distinction between 'time' and 'genesis'. Emerson's new American poet, in other words, does not begin with metres but with the argument (or vision, or story). But metres are indeed what he ends up with. For Emerson, sounding American was a matter of rediscovering the vitality in traditional, even Anglo-Saxon forms, never what Whitman called his own 'barbaric yawp'.

This is the point at which historians of American poetry begin to diverge – Emerson's apparent privileging of content over form and Whitman's rejection of conventional prosody. For Whitman, composing in metre would render American literary language dependent on English literary history. That would contradict the very principles, metaphysical and political, underpinning Whitman's poetry.

In terms of vision, the fusion of mysticism and politics, Whitman belongs with the other great English-language romantic poets, Shelley and Blake – just as Emily Dickinson belongs with the metaphysical poets Herbert and Crashaw. Perhaps the two branches of American poetry are the children of Whitman and the children of Dickinson.

It's easy to see Whitman as the fulfilment of Matthew Arnold's prophecy that poetry would one day replace religion. In American terms that translates easily into a species of religious or Whitmanian fundamentalism which regards any deviation from Whitman's vision as a mortal sin.

And here we have the beginnings of form as a political signifier in American poetry. *Leaves of Grass*, remember, appeared during the most nationalistic period in American literature. 'We want', shouted a character in Longfellow's *Kavanagh* (1849), 'a national literature altogether shaggy and unshorn, that shall shake the earth, like a herd of buffaloes thundering over the prairies.' Whitman made it his project to fill that demand. It was a massive sense of cultural inferiority that led many nineteenth-century American poets to defy whatever they took to be English – generally speaking, the highbrow, sophisticated and genteel. In the twentieth century, particularly in the wake of William Carlos Williams, traditional form began to be perceived as East Coast, urban, unconsciously loyal to England; free verse as truly American and democratic.

The received version of modernism, repeated endlessly in the introductions to textbook and anthologies, can be caricatured like this: expatriate American geniuses Ezra Pound and T. S. Eliot came to London in the first decade of this century and fearlessly smashed Romanticism and the pentameter. But the benighted English whose poetry was vague and sentimental and soft and went te tum te tum te tum wouldn't listen, driving Pound to Italy where he went mad and treasonous. From the wards of St Elizabeth's, Pound conferred the ring of St Peter on a poet named Charles Olson. Of course, the revolution was constantly under threat from 'reactionary' influences smuggled in by foreigners like Auden, but it surged forward toward postmodernism.

It's usually presented more elaborately, but that's the reductive and insidiously jingoistic gist of it. A typical example would be Louis Simpson's introduction to his 1978 book *A Revolution in Taste*, which aimed to simplify the situation for undergraduates:

> English writers use poetry as a means of discourse, they are conscious of the weight of the past and of their place in a literary tradition. Americans believe, as Wallace Stevens put it, that poetry is not a literary activity; it is a vital activity.

Or take Simpson again, flag-waving in a 1979 issue of *Poetry East*:

The American form of government, as Lincoln said, is experimental, and so is American poetry. It is as natural for an American poet to try new forms as for an Englishman not to.

I hope this is getting your backs up.

This is the version of events I was force-fed as a student in the seventies. Curiously, Simpson himself started out as a rather dull formalist and converted to Whitmanian fundamentalism in response to a huge poetry book that shook America in the mid-fifties and increased enormously poetry's cultural significance. If we look back to the fifties, we can spot the exact year it hit.

Between 1952 and 1959, Robert Creeley, then a relatively obscure avant-garde poet, published seven books and pamphlets of his own poetry. Six of the seven appeared in editions with a minuscule print run of 200 to 600 copies. Two years later his fortunes changed dramatically: in 1962 the New York publishing giant Scribners sensed a change in the market and brought out *For Love*, a collection of those very same poems; the first printing was over 6,000. Within ten years there would be 39,000 copies of this book in circulation.

What single event rocketed Creeley, and poets like him, to prominence?

'I saw the best minds of my generation destroyed by madness, starving, hysterical, naked' – Allen Ginsberg's *Howl* (1956). Its impact was unprecedented: to date there are 315,000 copies of the book in print. Its fame was more or less guaranteed when the San Francisco police confiscated copies of the book shortly after printing. I often think of that action by the San Francisco Collector of Customs turning the page to a line like 'who let themselves be fucked in the ass by saintly motorcyclists, and screamed with joy' as a turning point in American poetry. Within a very short time the book sold 50,000 copies. At the time, Kenneth Rexroth called *Howl* 'the confession of faith of the generation that is going to be running the world in 1965 and 1975'. Rexroth was a prophet.

I was born two years before *Howl* was published and the first question on an exam I sat to enter graduate school in 1976 was to identify the first line of that poem. In the seventies poets like me were asked to believe that the avant-garde poets of the fifties were opposing a bourgeois establishment which by our time had accepted the avant garde as a style and paid to be outraged. For us, Ginsberg was the establishment.

One notion that came and went in the seventies which I attribute to the influence of Ginsberg was the mystique of spontaneity. When I was first scribbling in the Bronx in the early seventies, the official line from the poets-in-residence was that rhyme and metre were rational impositions on honest, spontaneous thought. No one ever bothered to explain what was rational about them or just how long you had to think about something before it stopped being spontaneous. Ginsberg did a lot to promote this belief because it added to the Ginsberg myth. He always claimed to have written *Howl* in a white heat of rapid activity using Jack Kerouac's 'spontaneous bop prosody' which, he said, 'required an absolute, Zen-like absorption in the act of writing'. Anyone tempted to believe that should have a look at the Ginsberg Archives the poet bequeathed to Columbia University, at the drafting and redrafting of *Howl* recorded in his notebooks. In fact, the poem was composed slowly and laboriously over the course of six years.

But the event that consolidated Ginsberg's impact and ushered in the poetry boom was the publication of Donald Allen's anthology *The New American Poetry* in 1960, a much-publicized challenge to the authority of the *New Poets of England and America* collection put together two years earlier by Donald Hall, Robert Pack and, surprise, Louis Simpson. The heated literary controversy thus generated became known as the 'war of the anthologies'. There's no question as to who won. Allen set out to publicize the avant-garde, and (note the difference between the titles) purge the *Englishness* from the American reader's consciousness. England no longer existed.

He was remarkably successful: by the mid-sixties his anthology had gone through eight printings for a total of 40,000 copies – most of which, I need hardly tell you, were bought by universities. It was this anthology that linked, in the public's mind, the Beats with the movement known as Black Mountain – though *Howl* has about as much in common with Tennyson as it has with the poetry of Charles Olson.

And it shifted the subject matter of mainstream, or academic poetry. It was Lowell in 1959, who famously identified two 'competing' types of poetry and clearly he had in mind the challenge that Beat poets offered to traditional or 'academic' poets like himself. 'There is a poetry that can only be studied, and a poetry that can only be declaimed, a poetry of pedantry and a poetry of scandal.'

Lowell won the National Book Award for *Life Studies*, launching what came to be known as the confessional tendency in American poetry. In a draft for his acceptance speech he described the two poetries: 'The cooked, marvelously expert and remote, seems constructed as a sort of mechanical or catnip mouse for graduate seminars; the raw, jerry-built and forensically deadly seems often like an unscored libretto by some bearded but vegetarian Castro.'

After 1960, as a result of all this publicity, most of the avant-garde poets of the 1950s had little trouble finding trade presses to publish their books in printings they could only have dreamt about ten years earlier. Furthermore, the audience for all serious poetry, established as well as avant-garde, grew during the early 1960s. In one year, between 1963 and 1964, the total distribution of *Poetry* magazine (that's *Poetry* brackets *Chicago*, by the way) jumped by almost 50 per cent to just under 10,000. And throughout the seventies that figure grew and grew.

The average young poet starting out in the seventies stood a good chance of selling as many copies of his or her first book as T. S. Eliot had sold, forty years earlier, of *The Waste Land*.

Several other, non-artistic forces combined to increase the poetry audience. During the sixties:

1) The federal government gave support to libraries;
2) Typesetting had become much more expensive over the last thirty years. Print runs had to increase to keep down the unit price of each individual volume;
3) During the same period trade publishing houses grew into or were absorbed by large corporations and Knopf, Viking and Houghton Mifflin required respectable print runs to make

publication profitable. Today, these houses routinely print 4,000 copies of a new poetry book on their current lists, even for poets who've had little time to establish a following.

But what gave American poetry a truly public platform and cultural authority was, of course, the war. Vietnam created the counterculture which in its explosive growth absorbed the artistic avant-garde. When the war ended – for America, at least – in '73, the political fuel for the revolution dried up. Apart from the black and feminist powerbases it had helped nurture, the counterculture became a commercial exercise in nostalgia. By the seventies the former firebrands had settled down to become poets-in-residence. Ginsberg even founded his own poetry academy in Colorado: the Naropa Institute.

By far the largest poetry readerships in the seventies were ensconced in universities. A knock-on effect of the sixties poetry boom was the growth in the seventies of creative-writing programmes modelled on the venerable old international-writing programmes at Iowa, Yaddo and Breadloaf. Faced with the profusion of contemporary voices in print, academics had largely given up on the serious study of poetry written after Lowell. James Breslin put it like this: 'In the fifties criticism dictated to poetry like the husband in a patriarchal marriage – in the sixties they divorced and the husband lost all interest in the opposite sex.' While both creative writing programmes and the 'straight' academic study of English were housed in the same universities they had less and less to do with one another. The last person you'd expect to find at a campus poetry reading would be an English professor. Let's think of the English departments metastasizing into the academy proper – devoted to 'serious' scholarship – and the workshop, a kind of vocational school for poets. There were, last time I checked, well over two hundred and fifty graduate creative-writing programmes in America. Annually, hundreds of students win their MFAs by producing slim volumes of free-verse lyric poetry. They then go on to teach – guess what – creative writing. The effect is like a literary pyramid sales scam: nobody consumes the product but they sell shares in the company. It's not just poets and novelists, of course, it has been pointed out that the education system in America fabricates as many graduate painters and sculptors every five years as there were *people* in Florence in the fifteenth century.

In 1960 Donald Allen described as the unifying characteristic of his anthology 'a total rejection of all those qualities typical of Academic verse.' But in the seventies, with hundreds of officially 'qualified' poets flooding the trade houses with manuscripts, mainstream poetry was slowly colonized by a new kind of academic verse (not the academic poetry of the fifties – metrical poems about poems, or about foreign cities or Renaissance paintings steeped in world-weary irony, but free verse confessional lyrics, 'surrealism with a heart', epiphanies around the backyard barbecue, innumerable free verse poems about poems). Soul. Wind. Pain. Light . . .

The academic verse of the seventies was really workshop verse, and it evinced the values of those fifties poets who hitched a ride for two decades on the counterculture: a simple, stripped-down syntax and vocabulary (what Marianne Moore called 'plain American that dogs and cats can read'), a concentration on the image, without explicit moral interpretation, and the first-person perspective, even when the 'I' is disguised as 'You', you get the feeling the poet is talking to himself. An approach my friend Jo Shapcott once dismissed as 'I saw this and here's what I thought about it'. By the eighties there were so many of these dull epiphanies infesting the magazines Donald Hall called them 'McPoems'. Somehow, poetry's public voice had eroded in direct proportion to its explosive growth.

And to understand that problem we have to go back to the schoolroom, to a book called *Understanding Poetry* by the poet Robert Penn Warren and the critic Cleanth Brooks. It was published in 1938 and it's still in print. No other textbook in our century has exerted more influence on the way poetry's been taught.

The primary technique advocated by Brooks and Warren is close, analytic reading of the text, a technique as old as Aristotle's *Poetics*. Even today, most students do 'close reading' assignments following the techniques set forth by Brooks and Warren. But there was more to the New Critical agenda: poetry was a special kind of discourse, a means of communicating feeling and thought that could not be expressed in any other kind of language. Emphasis on the connotative and associative values of words at the expense of direct statement. Here was an American book that championed Eliot, Auden the Metaphysicals, for their complexity, ambiguity, their deployment of paradox – and made little or no mention of Whitman!

Understanding Poetry helped to persuade several generations of poets that poetry must be its own excuse for being, not an art which can or does communicate denotatively as well as connotatively, intellectually as well as imagistically. And it privileged the lyric poem because it was easier to teach.

It would have been the book Ginsberg, Bly, Plath and Rich. encountered as the official approach against which they launched their rebellion, but so deeply had it influenced their idea of what poetry was that the rebellion kept circling back to the lyric poem and the private epiphany.

Take the case of Robert Bly, one of the most influential poets of the sixties and seventies. You can see Bly's influence everywhere in the seventies – editing a magazine called the *Seventies* – and leading the movement of political poetry during the Vietnam War and one of the organizers of 'Poets Reading Against the Vietnam War'; Vietnam made Bly a public figure, most famously when he donated all the money he received for the National Book Award in 1968 to the anti-war group Resistance. Today, of course, he's more famous for *Iron John* and encouraging grown men to gallop naked through the woods beating drums. But there's a continuity there, a kind of fundamentalist faith in the collective unconscious, and in himself as its prophet. Since 1958 Bly has campaigned against any kind of formal measure, against any sophistication in syntax or vocabulary – all of which he equates with that bogeyman, reason – and for an American poetry *heavy with images from the unconscious*'.*

* The unconscious became an independent state in the twentieth century and its borders aren't very clearly established. They don't stamp your passport when you go there and we have only the artist's word that he or she has been. But any psychologist can tell you you can't consciously bulldoze your way into the unconscious.

Nevertheless, the surrealist imagery garnered from his translations of Neruda and Lorca powered his finest poems during the Vietnam period, poems like 'The Teeth Mother Naked At Last' or 'Counting the Small-Boned Bodies'.

> Let's count the bodies over again.
> If we could only make the bodies smaller,
> maybe we could fit
> a whole year's kill in front of us on a desk.

After 1973, however, Bly, like other poets in this mode, was forced back on himself for his subject, and his poetry begins to decline. So he becomes a guru: if the truth society requires lives exclusively in the depths of dream and emotion rather than in observable social interaction, we'll all need a guru to guide us to it. Enter Iron John. Without the bombers and the napalm, his elemental diction rings hollow. Bly, from the mid-seventies on, is full of spiritually profound gestures and pieties punctuated by copious exclamation marks.

Mud, snow, darkness, solitude. I hold Bly responsible for that paralysingly boring 'elemental' diction that characterized so much seventies poetry, reducing it to a kind of fridge-magnet poetry. In 1976 the poet Robert Pinsky identified the problem in his book *The Situation of Poetry*. He called for a return to 'the prose virtues . . . a drab, unglamorous group, including perhaps Clarity, Flexibility, Efficiency, Cohesiveness . . . a puritanical assortment of shrews. They do not as a rule appear in blurbs. And yet when they are courted by those who understand them – they can become not merely the poem's minimum requirement, but the poetic essence'.

Pinsky's criticism of seventies poetry is targeted on the prevailing poetic diction, and interior, submerged, 'surrealist' diction implying a particular elemental reality: 'breath', 'snow', 'blood', 'silence', 'eat', 'water' and most of all 'light' doing the wildly unexpected.

He refers to one recent book of poems (which he courteously leaves unnamed), which contains all of the words listed above, light 'drills' into eyes 'like a stream of liquid beads'; a 'little loaf of light' rises 'in the sea's dark pan'; a 'shard of light', in one of the run-on images which characterize all poetic dictions everywhere, is 'in the shape of an island from which dogs are leaping into the water' – but then, the poet muses, 'or maybe the light implodes'; there appear 'eels of shy light'; another person must 'go the rest of the way / by eating the light.' The blank, simple substances – snow, water, air – create a world where 'silence' reigns and 'eating' is the main, monumental process: 'we eat our way through grief and make it richer.' (As it turns out I had met the author of those lines, one Raphael Rudnik. Poor Rudnik, rocketed from obscurity to derision without even the promised fifteen minutes!) Pinsky improvises a poem in the mode: 'The silence of my / blood eats light like the / breath of future water'.

Although the lyric concentration on private travail and private epiphany diminished poetry's public voice for male poets, it provided an important starting point for feminists. It's an issue addressed by Adrienne Rich in her essay 'When We Dead Awaken'. She's said she discovered during the Vietnam years that politics was not something 'out there but something in here and of the essence of my condition'. And in her best-known book, *Diving into the Wreck* (1973), she seeks to dissolve the barriers 'between private and public, between Vietnam and lover's bed, between the deepest images we carry out of our dreams and the most daylight events out in the world.' Rich is one of the few poets to have emerged from the seventies with a truly commanding public voice. In response to Galway Kinnell's essay 'Poetry, Personality and Death' she wrote 'Poetry, Personality and Wholeness'. She agreed with Kinnell that certain male poets were on the right track in moving beyond mere personality toward a persona or an abstract 'I', but she felt that these were still an evasion. Only an inward look would authenticate the 'I', rather than idealize it, she argues, and she posits Emily Dickinson as a model.

If the two branches of American poetry are the line of Whitman and the line of Dickinson, the seventies saw the children of this broken home trying to reunite their parents. Where previously the Whitmanian 'I' was seen as the proper locus for a politicial poetry, in the seventies, I would argue, American poets moved gradually closer to the lapidary intensity of Dickinson.

A case in point is C. K. Williams, who moved from the formless, unpunctuated style of his second book, *I Am The Bitter Name*, in 1971 to forging his own unique form in his 1977 collection *With Ignorance*: a long line of roughly ten metrical feet. It looks like the American long line as practised by Ginsberg or Robinson Jeffers or Whitman – until you begin reading and find instead of the declamatory style of those poets a complex, even convoluted syntax full of interruptions and emotional fine-tunings.

> Until I asked her to please stop doing it and was astonished to
>   find that she not only could
> but from the moment I asked her in fact would stop doing it,
>   my mother, all through my childhood,
> when I was saying something to her, something important,
>   would move her lips as I was speaking
> so that she seemed to be saying under her breath the very words
>   I was saying as I was saying them.

The dithyrambs of Whitman and Ginsberg are not conducive to reconsideration or self-doubt. 'The open shirted buddies of the universe', as a friend of mine once called them, seem to be shouting at us from the heights of enlightenment. Williams is trying to represent the tonal modulations, which is to say the music, of a liberal analytical voice. And Williams has grown steadily more formal since the seventies, to the point of including a villanelle in his most recent collection.

The precedent that springs to mind isn't Whitman but Whitman's model, the young Wordsworth, who sought to forge a moral and political instrument out of poetic diction and description: vivid, exact and unflinching description of the circumstances of the dispossessed (Vietnam vets, pornographic models, suicides – the equivalent of Wordsworth's vagrants and leech-gatherers). His version of the long line impedes our rush to judgement – Look again, he says. Think again.

It's a technique inspired in part by the great formalist and virtuoso of description Elizabeth Bishop. The neglect of Bishop by the critical establishment of the sixties is part of the Whitmanian poet's denial of the Dickinson line, the line of American formalism. Louis Simpson, quoted earlier, is particularly touchy about the 'Auden generation'. W. H. Auden's residence in the States after 1939 had an enormous influence among east-coast poets who were attracted to his sophistication, his ear, and his wit.

In the postwar years American poets returned to traditional measures. Some of the younger poets, including Bishop, Richard Wilbur, James Merrill, Anthony Hecht, were called New Formalists, a term that returned in the seventies applied to a whole new generation of poets. They absorbed and transformed many modernist principles, such as the centrality of the image, but they were anxious to get the rough beast buried; understandably, considering the political record of the modernists. 'Tradition' offered an escape from ideology.

All of these poets I just listed are recorded as poets of the fifties; *all* of them published their best work in the seventies.

1970   Elizabeth Bishop's *Complete Poems*
1972   James Merrill's *Braving the Elements*
1976   Bishop's *Geography III*
          Merrill's *Divine Comedies*
          Wilbur's *The Mind Reader*
1977   Anthony Hecht's *Millions of Strange Shadows*

In my opinion, the last four books mentioned contain some of the century's greatest poems. Bishop's 'Crusoe in England', Merrill's 'Book of Ephraim's Wilbur's 'Mind Reader'. Richard Wilbur has been the Whitmanian's whipping boy since 1960. One of the dimmer beacons of American Lit Crit., Leslie Feidler, complained in 1964 that he found in Wilbur 'no personal source anywhere, as there is no passion and no insanity . . .' (insanity was *in* in 1964). There's an element of truth there, though it's worth considering why Wilbur never played the confessional card. He began writing poems in 1943 as 'a momentary stay against confusion' while on active service with the 36th Infantry Division. Having experienced Monte Cassino,

Anzio and the Siegfried Line firsthand he must have been rather unimpressed by the next generation's production of private hells.

In 1976 Wilbur confronted his own technical facility in poems like 'The Writer', 'Cottage Street 1953' and 'The Mind Reader', a long dramatic monologue delivered by an alcoholic Italian psychic who poses as an oracle. He can't predict the future, he can only read minds.

James Merrill in 1976 published *Divine Comedies*. There are three things to note about James Merrill: he's outrageously wealthy, well read, and gay. Divine: a fruitful, if risky, area for study would be how the competing influences of the straight and gay 'voice' in American poetry manifest as the earnest, serious, plain and sincere tone vs. the ornamental, arch, mischievous, ironic and deflating – what Susan Sontag detailed perhaps a little too exhaustively in her 1964 'Notes on Camp'. Neither tendency is the exclusive province of the gay or the straight, of course. After all, there's absolutely nothing camp or arch about Whitman – at least as far as he was concerned – whereas it's second nature to straight poets like Kenneth Koch or Anthony Hecht.

Divine Comedies ends with 'The Book of Ephraim', a long narrative poem, the first instalment in fact, of a three-volume poem, *The Changing Light at Sandover*, a 17,000-line epic, the most unpredictable and extravagant poem in American history, which rivals great poems of the past in its scope, length and complexity, or the prose of Proust or Nabokov.

Ephraim begins on a note of urgency:

> Admittedly I err by undertaking
> This in its present form. The baldest prose
> Reportage was called for, that would reach
> The widest public in the shortest time.

He goes on to tell how in 1955 he and his lover David Jackson are playing with a Ouija board in the upstairs room of their house in Connecticut, when suddenly the upturned teacup they are using for a pointer is commandeered by the soul of one of Caligula's murdered slaves, who was also, conveniently, gay. The spirit, Ephraim, answers their questions instantly, and largely in rhyme and metre, but, economically, without punctuation, in capital letters and using abbreviations and ampersands:

> ARE U XTIANS
> We thought so. WHAT A COZY CATACOMB

As the sessions continue, Ephraim introduces Merrill and Jackson to the geography and politics of the invisible world. They get to meet the Archangel Michael and various other luminaries. The sessions go on for years and as their friends die they pop up on the Ouija board. These include the avant-garde filmmaker Maya Deren and Auden. And as chapters of the poem get published, everyone from Alexander Pope to Wallace Stevens crowds in to comment.

Of course, we think of Yeats, who claimed to have contacted and drawn on the assistance of 'the other side'. And Merrill refers to the attraction of the 'bedevilling couplet' and it's clear to this reader, at least, that Merrill's supernatural familiars are in part metaphors for the shaping forces of verse technique. On another level it's a device that enables Merrill to compose a serious yet witty summation of his lifelong concerns. But the most remarkable thing, for me, is that Merrill swore to the end of his life that the whole thing happened just as he reported it.

But there's a secret history, another version of the seventies, we're only beginning to discern: throughout the seventies unbeknownst to me or my colleagues on the *Chicago Review* there were two distinct groups who would like to style themselves *pockets of resistance*. Both groups were outside the academic closed shop of the writing programme and took some time to get themselves noticed.

Because of the inescapable vectors or forces I mentioned at the beginning, cooked and raw, it's pretty clear both sides have to line up as one or the other.

In this corner we have the New Formalists or as they call themselves, Expansionists – journalists, psychiatrists, novelists, feminist philosophers and business executives who wrote sonnets, stories, sometimes entire novels in rhyme and metre. They published in their own obscure little magazines through the decade and then, in 1978, Charles Martin published *Room for Error*, and in 1979 Tim Steele published *Uncertainties and Rest*. Naturally both books were unreviewed. But then the journalists got wind of it – 'movements' make good copy – and when Brad Leithauser's *Hundreds of Fireflies* was published in '82 it was reviewed everywhere as a New Formalist debut. Moreover, these poets were popular, if not always populist. Vikram Seth's novel written in the stanza form of Pushkin's Eugene Onegin, *The Golden Gate*, became something of a middlebrow sensation, receiving notices everywhere including *Newsweek*, a magazine that never reviews poetry. Black poets like Rita Dove and June Jordan, lesbian and gay poets like Marilyn Hacker and Bruce Bawer, realized the political advantage of reaching an audience outside the hothouse atmosphere of the workshop. They were united in their departure from, or announced rejection of, the free verse confessional lyric in favour of formal and narrative poems. Rhyme was back! Demonstrable skill was back! It was a gauntlet thrown before the mainstream.

And in this corner we have the language poets, the true heirs of the avant-garde mantle. Who are they? Lyn Hejinian, Bob Perelman, Clark Coolidge, Ron Silliman and Bruce Andrews. What do they sound like? Here's an example by Charles Bernstein:

> Mass of van contemplation to intercede crush of
> Lots of loom 'smoke out', merely
> complicated by the first time something and don't.
> Long last, occurrence of bell, altitude, attitude of.
> The first, at this moment, aimless, aim. To the
> point of inordinate asphalt – lecture, entail.

Whatever you can say about that, it's not mainstream. Taking up language poet Bob Perelman's *The Marginalization of Poetry* we find him denouncing MFA writing programmes and mainstream poetry in *exactly* the same language we find in New Formalist critiques. Perelman says language poets were united in

1 breaking the automatism of the poetic 'I' and its naturalized voice;

2 foregrounding textuality and formal devices;
3 using or alluding to Marxist or poststructural theory in order to open the present to critique and change.

Substitute the word 'narrative' for 'Marxist or poststructural theory' and you have exactly the stated aims of the New Formalists. That's not all they have in common. Both groups have a genius for self-mythologizing. There are plenty of 'histories of the movement' from both camps. And both groups harp on about the hostility they encountered when they launched their revolutions.

> During this period, American poetry has been dominated by writing workshops and creative writing departments with large networks of legitimation – publishing, awards, reviews, extensive literary connections.

Interestingly, Mr Perelman's book is published by Princeton University Press. So his days in the wilderness are over. If 'mainstream' means accepted and canonized, then language poetry is in the vanguard of the mainstream, a movement tailor-made for the academy. Consider:

1 'Language writing' as a self-conscious movement, is, Perelman argues, over, so it's a bit of literary history. Now academics can hold conferences on it;
2 The poetry is extremely resistant so it requires professional decoding assistance from a critic;
3 Academics respond to language poets because they speak their language. The manifestos read something like this:

> The cipheral text involves the replacement of a traditionally 'readerly' function . . . by a first order experience of graphemes, their material tension and relationships and their sign potentiality as substance, hypo-verbal units simultaneously pushing towards, yet resisting contextual significations.

In other words it doesn't mean anything. In short, for the first time in history a kind of poetry has been created by the critical apparatus designed to interpret it. Perelman himself puts it best:

'Language writing was easy enough to subsume under the category of theory or postmodernism as part of a large tendency attacking self, reference, and history.'

Two academic critics have come along to champion their respective teams. Marjorie Perloff, in the words of Expansionist poet Tom Disch, has a relationship toward the 'postmodern' poetry she champions much like the relationship of Dona Elvira to Don Giovanni in Mozart's opera. She has a passionate enthusiasm for its potential that the repeated experience of its unworthiness never dampens.

The poststructuralist apologists for language poetry are the spitting image of the New Critical apologists for the academic poetry of the forties and fifties. Consider: a critical style coterminous with, if not actually preceding, the poetry itself – it all matches up – for rejection of bourgeois affect read 'affective fallacy', for 'breaking the automatism of the poetic "I" and its naturalised voice' read 'impersonalism', for 'Bob Perelman' read 'Bob Warren'.

Helen Vendler is a more conventional critic. Like Harold Bloom, she started out writing about the Romantics and then deigned to notice some contemporary writing. Bear in mind that Bloom's writing on Ashbery led immediately to Ashbery's *Self-Portrait in a Convex Mirror* (1975) winning the National Book Award for poetry, the Pulitzer Prize for poetry, and the National Book Critics Circle Prize. Fame and critical attention are a black hole from whose gravitational field not even mediocrity can escape.

But no academic critic has come to rescue the Expansionists. Despite all their attempts to generate journalistic interest and woo the American common reader, they failed to produce from their ranks a theory or manifesto attractive to the academy. I have noticed, though, that the mainstream of American verse grew steadily more formal through the nineties. Poets who couldn't rub two rhymes together in 1977 are now writing villanelles.

In conclusion I'd like to ask whose version of the seventies will prevail? Who controls literary history? The common reader? The public buys what they want, but the record of what they want, what gets anthologized and reprinted, is controlled by the academy.

Otherwise we'd be examining American poetry in the light of Longfellow, not Whitman. My co-editor at the *Chicago Review* who had never heard of Seamus Heaney has written an article that concludes

> It has long been known in America that the audience for poetry is dependent on the culture of the universities and its illusion of a Common Reader has died a slower death in Britain . . .

In America the critical theory of the day shapes contemporary poetry. Awards are given with an eye for such critical theory and money goes to that poetry which reflects established values or critical theory. When we look back on seventies American poetry in twenty years' time, I predict (pessimistically) that it will be called the Language Era. But it will be called the Language Era by Academics. And here's the good news: you don't have to listen to them.

May I Make A Suggestion?

Five rules for the newly enrolled poet

Students sometimes enroll in poetry classes in order to learn what they take to be a set of formal rules for writing verse, so in my workshops I'm at pains to emphasize that there are no rules for writing poetry. Or rather there are innumerable sets of unforeseeable rules; imagine a form of chess incorporating all the known manoeuvres with their infinite permutations but add as legitimate moves licking the chess pieces one by one or scattering petals on the chessboard or slapping your opponent with a rubber chicken. 'Welcome,' I say, 'this is a workshop for poets of all levels.' 'Are you a genius?' I ask them. 'If so, please stay at home and write your opus. You don't go to the doctor's to show them how fit you are. You don't take your car to the garage so the mechanics can admire it. You don't take a poem to a workshop if you don't want advice.'

Over the years I've noticed that good poetry is thoroughly unpredictable. It always surprises. But bad poetry is always bad in the same way. So I've collected a set of suggestions which I advise the inexperienced to follow for six months. After that, I tell them, drop them and follow your instinct.

1. *READ IT* . . . Literature is a conversation. You have to know what and how poets are writing before you enter that dialogue. Imagine a musician who doesn't listen to music or a dinner guest who insists on talking whilst refusing to listen. Bad poetry is not unrelated to bad manners. Collect poems that move you and read

them carefully. Poets dream of exerting an influence on other writers. It's only polite to steal everything you can.

2. *SAY IT* . . . Don't be 'unspeakable'. That is, use ordinary word order – the kind of sentences one would use when speaking to be understood. Test your poem by speaking it aloud and write as if you're actually speaking to someone. Don't, for example, distort the normal word order to force a rhyme or sound unspeakably 'poetic', as in 'He drew his sword the scabbard from' or 'Down the boulevard I did stroll'. This gives your writing an affected antiquity – rather like wearing a monocle. Similarly, avoid using unspeakably 'modern' sentence fragments; 'whistlestream brownpour contentsigh' is not a daring and sophisticated way of describing a cup of tea. It's just silly.

3. *SHOW IT* . . . Whenever you want to say something, stop. Don't. Show it instead. The sad fact is that nobody wants to know what you think. They want to discover what they think. If you show what you mean through concrete imagery, readers will discover the meaning for themselves. An idea is more effectively communicated if you can see, touch, hear, smell or taste it. A colt kicking and bucking in a frosty paddock before dawn, the newsagent opening his shop, looking up into the sun and bursting into an out-of-tune rendition of Bizet's 'March of the Toreadors' – the word 'joy' is a vague and inadequate way to label these specific instances.

4. *LISTEN* . . . What makes a person a bore in conversation? Droning on about himself? Or about people you don't know? Preaching? Telling you what to think? All these things make for boring poetry too, so listen to yourself and consider the impatient reader. More importantly, listen to the poem you're writing. If you've made your mind up what you're going to say and stick to it regardless of whatever surprise the writing has in store for you, you're practising the art of advertising.

5. *SHAPE IT* . . . I use the term 'integritas' to describe a synthesis – the way in which a poem is established as all one thing – a term I've borrowed from James Joyce. 'Integritas' is the first step to what

Joyce calls 'radiance'. When you play with the boundaries of the poem, you exploit an irresistible human instinct: just as we stare ink blots in a Rorschach test into the shapes of clouds or people or animals, we long to wrest coherence from the structure of a poem. The reader is willing to go halfway to accommodate you – but no more.

The Questionnaire

'*Which poet or poets, have you been most surprised to enjoy?*'

Personification: no ideas but with wings. Long before Wordsworth rejected it as a contraption of poetic diction, Pope lampooned the Augustan version with the toast 'Set Bacchus from his glassy prison free'. But remember, in the cult of Dionysus god and wine were indistinguishable in *Theoinus*, the 'god-wine' – in Haiti, according to experimental filmmaker and voodoo priestess Maya Deren, death is not a dying man or a corpse. It's the shadowy Baron Ghede de la Croix sporting his top hat and broken sunglasses. Lately, I've been interested in poems where personification lies somewhere between ironic trope and supernatural encounter. I've been hunting the *Melancholy*.

Look at Dürer's sulky angel bored with her educational toys. Looks like she's waiting for someone. Not Milton, though. He seeks 'divinest Melancholy / Whose saintly visage is too bright / To hit the sense of human sight' whom he asks to 'Dissolve [him] into ecstasies'. Not Marvell either. He's pursuing something far more intense: 'Magnanimous Despair alone / Could show me so divine a thing, / Where feeble Hope could ne'er have flown, / But vainly flapped its tinsel wing'. And certainly not Keats. Who'd mistake this glum creature for his terrifying goddess lying in wait in her dark sanctum deep within the temple of Delight, surrounded by the cloudy souls of those hunters who've burst joy's grape against their palettes and tasted the sadness of her might? Me neither.

Was Keats Japanese? Japanese tourists at his Hampstead shrine might suspect he knew something of *mono no aware*, that exquisite sadness induced by the sight of clouds passing in the sky, by the cherry blossom that blooms for three days before scattering. The Heian master Kukai taught that only such fragile mortal beauty can reveal the Buddha's truth: all that lives must suffer and die. See Paz: *Tres Momentos de la Literatura Japonesa* . . . That's Octavio Paz, who translated Basho and maintained that Lorca absorbed this appetite from haiku . . . That's F. Garcia Lorca, who warned that the *Duende* is neither Muse nor Angel.

These are important distinctions. Dürer's mopey soul is an impostor. She's *Depression* or some minor spirit suffering from that complaint, a condition which drains significance from the world. Its polar (as in bipolar) opposite is that surfeit of meaning which feeds *Melancholy* – or, as anyone who's dined in the company of poets will attest, her hideous bat-winged sister *Paranoia*.

INTERVIEWS

Interview with John Wall, 1996

Can you begin by telling us a little about your cultural background?
Can we classify you as British, Irish, or American?

I'll tell you what I think in terms of my poetry. My heritage is Irish, Catholic and proletarian. You can't shake any of those things, no matter how hard you try. But I can't locate in myself any trace of nationalism or patriotism or class allegiance, which is to say I feel a bit of a trespasser everywhere.

But you grew up in New York.

Yes. My parents emigrated from Ireland in the fifties and I grew up in the South Bronx, in a Spanish-speaking neighbourhood. It was a dangerous place to live even in the sixties and I didn't leave the Bronx until the late seventies. I want to avoid overdramatizing this. I wasn't tough and I attribute my survival to the fact that I kept off the streets. I knew people who died in grotesquely violent ways.

The Bronx figures prominently in Errata. *Are those poems based on personal experience?*

You see, that's one of those questions that makes me uncomfortable with the whole interview situation. I feel very strongly that my personality, a precise representation of me, doesn't really come into it. Borges has a story in which a twentieth-century Frenchman manages to reproduce Don Quixote word for word in sixteenth-century Spanish. And Borges, or the narrator, claims this new work is superior to the original because it was infinitely more difficult to produce. But the words are identical. Would the words on the pages of my books be magically transformed if you discovered I was, in fact, Japanese? For me the answer is a qualified 'no' because my poems are not about me. They're about you, the reader and the reader's reaction.

A 'qualified' no?

There's a margin where the facts of one's biography and the expectations of the reader bleed together into the context of the work. That's where the poem really exists – in that space between. I suppose that's why so much of what I write questions any uncomplicated assumption of identity. It's not that I'm being 'impersonal' in Eliot's sense. And certainly not in any Derridean sense. On the contrary.

Interesting you should mention Borges. The way he mythologizes the Southside slums of Buenos Aires reminds me of some of the poems in Errata, *'City of God', for example.*

I'll go along with that. I still dream about the Bronx. I suppose it's like an experience of war. Except in my case I spent the war hiding in a foxhole. The Bronx is important to me because of the genii of the place, its local gods . . .

Music, Sex, and Drink, as you told Poetry Review.

(laughs) The very fellows. They've been spotted in London, too.

Your work is virtually unknown in the States. Someone has called you the best-kept secret in American poetry. Why did you come to Britain? Did it have anything to do with poetry?

No. Purely personal reasons. But I've always been something of a contrarian and much of the American poetry I was reading at that time – especially the poetry most esteemed by critics – seemed very insipid to me. Surrealism seemed too easy . . .

You mean people like Ashbery?

Well, I actually went through an Ashbery stage – something that seems hard to believe now. I never published any of it. I'm not the least bit interested in that mode of poetry now. I was also very much into Stevens, but I took him too seriously, as if he were a kind of philosopher. Now I see what I took to be an encoded but rigorous ontology in his work is a red herring – his ministry is delight, not knowledge. And I was force-fed Black Mountain at university. In 1977 I started a PhD in English at the University of Chicago because I loved poetry and I was naive enough to be shocked when I found that the canon of modern poetry is not based on taste, on the excellence of this or that poet, but on something like the law of gravity. The mass of critical study already adhering to a poet attracts more and more study – maybe because there's less risk involved for the critic. The great modernist self-promoters like Pound and Olson were aware of this, and helped to initiate their own personality cults.

You rejected Pound?

No. No. I learned a lot from him. But he was the P. T. Barnum of his movement. Experimental modernism has been institutionalized for a century now. It's still using the same tired set of gestures and it no longer seems liberating.

So you turned to British models?

Let's say Irish. I never had much time for the Movement, if that's what you mean, and very little for British modernism – I was fascinated by Bunting and David Jones, and I still am, but they strike me as brilliant eccentrics, like Hopkins, only bigger. Then I found in Derek Mahon, and behind him MacNeice, a voice that engaged the whole of one's consciousness without resorting to any theories or manifestos. It used a richly varied diction and syntax. It could be witty and ride a razor edge of irony, and in the next line break your heart or fill you with wonder. And in these islands, poets never quite renounced traditional form to the extent they did in America. That means a lot to me, the singing line.

That was my next question. You're known for your facility with form. I've read several articles in which you come out in favour of the American New Formalists. Are you a New Formalist?

No. No room for membership cards in my wallet. It's funny, though. There I was writing formal poetry in the wilderness until 1975 when I left, and that was the very year. New Formalism seemed to break in the States. Maybe it's a blessing. I think I'm trying to do something very different with form. I have a lot of respect for what they try to do – Dana Gioia, Tim Steele and the rest – I certainly share their impatience with the institution of the free verse confessional lyric, on the one hand, and that sort of worthy fundamentalist modernism on the other. But I'm more concerned with the unconscious effect of form on the poet. The more resistant the medium – whether marble or metre – the more negotiation is required. You have to compromise what you originally intended to say – which is always more likely to be full of self-deception, prejudice and cliché – and it's in that negotiation that discovery takes place. So it's as much about surrender as 'mastery' of form. For me 'form' is the link with the oral tradition, with a memorizable shape. I think of Leonardo warning artists to keep their compositions 'provisional' until they hit upon a radiant form, and warning against a method which would tie their creative process down to the original commitment. He said the painter should be ready to change course at any moment, like the poet. Negotiation with the form helps me keep the poem fluid for as long as I can, so the 'better idea' can reveal itself. But let's not get carried away with this formal question. I write an awful lot of free verse, too, you know.

There's been a renewal of interest in poetry in the British media and you seem to have featured in a lot of this. Tell us about the 'New Generation poets', for instance.

Well, I'd rather not. But since you ask, the 'New Generation' was a confused attempt by publishers to promote their poetry lists by invoking the powers of a London public-relations firm called Colman Getty. So you had senior poets like Michael Longley, for example, selecting the poets – most of whom wrote serious, 'literary' poetry – and Colman-Getty and the media representing us as 'the new rock and roll'. In other words, it was a horrible embarrassment and the sooner it's forgotten the better. But to address the first part of your question, there has indeed been an increased awareness of poetry in popular consciousness here in Britain and Ireland. But I think performance poets are the real beneficiaries of this.

But I've seen you read and you read from memory, like a performance poet but without the theatricality. Why do you choose to do that?

Because I can. Why would I choose to look down into a book if I could do otherwise? The point is I'm striving for a memorizable form and reading from memory tests the poem.

I wonder if this relates to your work as a musician. You play traditional Irish music and you've recorded a jazz CD with the Scottish poet Don Paterson. You've also written about Irish music, blues and Greek folk music in the 'O'Ryan's Belt' section of Errata, *but is there also a structural or compositional connection between these musical forms and your poetry?*

The short, honest answer is 'no'. But I've been asked the question before and I conceded, just as a point of interest, that a memorizable form in traditional music – like a jig – has a lot in common with, say, a sonnet. Both have predictable shapes that resonate with every other jig or sonnet written down the centuries, both fit snugly in the mind's hand, and both forms permit for infinite variations. But there's nothing programmatic about it. I just grew up hearing this music, rejected it and rediscovered it in my twenties. I held off writing about it until *Errata* because I wanted to understand what it meant to me . . .

To stave off the charge of sentimentality?

Exactly, I knew if I was patient I'd find in it a vantage point from which I could explore tradition, politics and habit. And of course, the stories carry their own importance.

What strikes me as particularly unique is your use of metaphor. In a recent article in the TLS, *Hugo Williams compares your poem 'The Break', a true story of Siamese-twin musicians, to Paul Muldoon's 'Truce', and he says that you reverse a trend in contemporary poetry. You 'integrate meaning and metaphor by looking at every decision from both sides of the equation, then judge what is best for the poem.'*

Hugo said that? Well, it's flattering to be mentioned in the same breath as Muldoon, but I'm not sure what he means. If he means that I don't have a programme, that I don't go about writing poems according to a system, I'm with him there.

Sean O'Brien and Cathal Dallat have bracketed your work with Ian Duhig's and Don Paterson's. In their work and in yours I've noticed a tremendous volume of cultural allusion – not only literary and historical allusions to high culture, but to popular culture as well. Is this the makings of a school or a movement? Could it be said that you're postmodernists?

I suppose it could be said, but I wouldn't know what it meant. You're winding me up here, right? Forgive me – readers of this interview may not be familiar with your reputation as a leading light in contemporary electro-acoustic music – but in your own work you use digital sampling – exclusively – so your work is composed of snippets from sources as diverse as Shostakovitch, and madrigals, and Anthony Braxton. In the same way, though to a lesser extent, I'll drop an entire line from Pope or Ralegh into a poem. Now that's just the sort of technique an arts journalist might want to label postmodernist. But I've worked with you and I know there's much more depth to your work than that formal designation would suggest. As I said before, I don't subscribe to movements. Movements are only promotional rackets anyway. But I'm flattered that anyone sees fit to include me with Paterson and Duhig. They seem to me among the best young poets writing on this island. What you identify is probably something we all get from Muldoon, and Joyce before him, and it's probably part of the contemporary British or Irish zeitgeist. There's a trend here toward a phony accessibility which I find extremely patronizing. For me, all information is fair game. And Western civilization is a posh shop with the security cameras turned off.

One last question. There's a mystical or religious element in your work – often treated in an arch or ironic way – but it's a prevailing theme. And it's linked to ideas about language and eroticism. I'm thinking here of your more rhetorical, 'metaphysical' poems like 'Pentecost': 'Though we command the language of desire / The voice of ecstasy is not our own.'

I need to answer this carefully because a word like 'mysticism' is often equated with woolliness or imprecision. It may not be the right word at all. What I'm trying to get at in those poems is an adversary idiom, an alternative to theory, one situated in the body, in presence. They're the most formal poems for that reason – they stick in the memory because the words are arranged in a kind of dance. In 'Pentecost' – and poems like it – I'm saying that the most intense and emotional experience breaks open the crust of language like the dark crust of a hot coal. But if I say any more I'll be explaining my poems, which is like explaining a joke or telling you the butler did it.

Yeah. We can't have that. Thank you.

Interview with Conor O'Callaghan, 1997

I'd like to begin by asking you to say something about your background.

My father was from Belfast, my mother was from Tralee, and they came over to the States in '49–'50, and I was born in 1954 in the Bronx. But somewhere between the ages of one and four we tried to move back again, so I lived briefly in Belfast and Tralee as a child. As a matter of fact, we lived right across the street from where Ciaran Carson lives now. Then we moved back and we lived in the South Bronx. I don't want to over-dramatize the South Bronx, but I'm here talking to you now because I kept my head down. Once, long before my family emigrated, that area was predominantly Irish. In fact the area that I grew up in was known in the heyday of the recording of Irish traditional music as the 'Reel Factory' because there were a lot of tunes coming out of the area. But mostly where I grew up was a black and Puerto Rican neighbourhood, and we were part of a white minority in a black majority.

My parents played a little Irish music, and my mother sang. My father was also fond of recitations, so there was a lot of stuff like the dreaded Robert Service in the house. I heard a lot of that. But, although he left school at fifteen or so, he kept a lot of books around the house. He was an autodidact. There were a lot of anthologies of poetry. So I fell in love, as many young poets do, with the work of Dylan Thomas, among others. In those days the anthologies in the States, the older paperbacks edited by people like Oscar Williams, incorporated a lot of British and some Irish poets. So you could buy Austin Clarke or Ted Hughes or Dylan Thomas in those anthologies.

You worked for a time as poetry editor for Chicago Review, *and published an American collection. What is the poetry publishing culture like in America?*

I didn't publish a full collection in America. It was a little volume called *Slivers* which was more in the way of a chapbook, and was in fact never properly distributed. I'm sure it's still wrapped in cling-film under my publisher's desk in Chicago, where I found myself accidentally editing the poetry part of the *Chicago Review*. I enjoyed doing it. I 'discovered' a number of poets. It was exciting to be able to push work that excited me. Poetry in the States is just overwhelming. There are over two hundred and fifty creative-writing programmes, all of those people publishing slim volumes of verse that hardly anyone reads. It's strange to say this, it's the opposite of censorship but just as oppressive. If someone can be silenced by the armed guard at the door saying no one can speak or whisper, then someone can be silenced because everyone is screaming. It's all very Balkanized, very tribalized.

Signs and signatures are recurring concerns in early poems like 'Smith', and in the more recent poem 'L' you have a driving tester tell you 'It's all a question of giving – proper – signals'. Is there a furtive semiology at work in your poems?

I was doing a PhD at the University of Chicago, and had the honour of being asked to leave the room by Paul de Man. I found myself immersed in all this theory, and many of the concerns must have seeped into what I was writing. But looking back on my work, these concerns preceded my acquaintance with Derrida & Co. I was always fond of literary hoaxes. The fake Welsh translations in *Shibboleth* are very old. When I was at university I attended a few meetings of the Jung Foundation – God knows why – and I remember dropping a reference to a North African Gnostic belief that physical beings are all 3D hieroglyphics in an infinite text being written by God. Of course I made it up. The thing is, I later read it in one of their papers reported as fact. I love that sort of thing, like the conspirators in Borges's story who forge entries in the encyclopedia.

I began to think of it as the opposite to literature. I thought I'd do a degree in literature because I loved literature, then I realized that my colleagues hated literature. It's like saying that I decided to do vivisection because I loved animals. It's not the same thing, is it? They're not interested in literature, and they also despise actual living working writers. As writers we have no illusions about ourselves. We're ordinary men. We're not bards or special people. And yet when a writer is in a room with a critic, the critic develops an inferiority complex that he tends to overcompensate for. The critic thinks, 'I am a real scholar, this person is a paid entertainer.' I certainly miss the intellectual energy of theory, I enjoy the mental energy one expends unravelling these obfuscations in the same way that I enjoy a good run. But it's not the same as being intellectually rigorous.

In one of your most celebrated poems, 'Machines', you come to the conclusion that 'The cyclist, not the cycle, steers'. Would you say that you have a heightened sense of poetry's artifice?

I do. But that line, 'The cyclist, not the cycle, steers', is only half the truth. When you're working with a resistant form, you negotiate with form, and negotiation allows for serendipity. So it's only half true to say 'The cyclist, not the cycle, steers'.

But it begins, or should begin, as a conscious act. You have no mystical pretensions as a poet?

Well you see now, if someone were to ask you a question like 'Do you believe in God?' there's something almost rude about that question for an intellectual. It merely reduces it to a question of semantics. There's nothing mystical about the work. The muse, what's the muse? The muse I believe is an expression for the unconscious. It's an acceptable term. It's an allegorical term, like Socrates always referring to the gods in a similar way I think. I don't use the term the muse, but I understand its use, I understand what it means.

You have said that the strongest influences on your work have been pre-twentieth century. Who, and how does that work?

Donne, Herbert the metaphysical poets. Shakespeare! I'm also very interested in the convention of the conversation poem as practised by Wordsworth and Coleridge. It can be epistolary, narrative and dramatic all at the same time. But why do poets only ever cite poets as influences? I've learned as much from the syntax of Defoe or John Lyly as I have from verse.

Your work has also been linked with contemporary American formalists like Richard Wilbur and Anthony Hecht. How accurate is that?

That's very flattering. I hope it's accurate. I'm a great admirer of both Hecht and Wilbur. I think Wilbur's a great poet. He has such a good ear. I think he gets ignored. I'm a great admirer of Hecht as well, but I think people would want to take a second look at Richard Wilbur. He often has the one point to make and he keeps on making it about things of this world, the quotidian. His is an anti-mystical, an anti-idealist stance. There's a poem of his called 'The Mindreader' which is a very great poem.

You're not so strict on form as Hecht or Wilbur. A poem like 'Alas, Alice' uses the possible rhyming structure in prose stanzas.

Well that's because the poem is only rhythm – so much so that it seemed unnecessary to lineate it as verse. I've sometimes approached it at the opposite angle: the title poem of *Errata* was originally written in prose and worked on until I discovered lines taking shape. Coming back to the thing about form and experimentalism, I find that people always talk about influences, but you know, negative influence is very powerful. I think Charles Olson is a very great influence on my work, in that I don't see the point. I find his poetry boring and I find his critical writing absurd.

On a topical point, Allen Ginsberg died recently. He was somebody who made a career out of opposition to mainsteam poetry as embodied by Hecht and Wilbur. How do you value his work?

It's possible now, in American schools, to take an exam on Allen Ginsberg and fail it. There's a market for being opposed to mainstream culture. I don't want to say anything about poor Ginsberg now that he's dead, but there was a time when he'd shock everybody at poetry readings by taking off his clothes and running around the stage. Towards the end of his life, he would sit there quietly in his tweed suit, while people would give lectures on his work. Early on he liked to give the impression that poems like *Howl* were written rapidly in a fever of Beat improv, when in fact they were carefully worked out in successive drafts. And I have no problem with any of this, my only problem is with the self-delusion involved when artists/writers/poets believe they are opposed to mainstream culture and they are just playing their part. That romantic idea, as it stands, began with advertising. 'Throw that away, and buy this. That is the old style, this is the new style.' That's consumerism. You can't be an oppositional poet unless you abandon the concept of the avant-garde.

But your work is not intensely formal in the way that Hecht's and Wilbur's is?

But I realize that I can move away from it too. I'll deliberately mess it up in the way that a drummer 'drops a bomb' – throws in a little extra polyrhythm. Any musician knows this: you have to create a recognizable pattern, a groove, to provide a ground against which a figure can be perceived. I think what you're saying is that I don't write straight sonnets. In fact I have done – take 'The Present' in *Shibboleth*. It's just typographically disguised. I do believe verse is an aural form. For me it's a musical form. So I don't ever count syllables because I don't believe we hear syllables, we hear beats. There's something absurd about syllabics in English. The haiku may be a great form in Japanese but in English you have to forgo the natural rhythms of the language for a Dalek-like monotony.

You work as a musician. How different are these two jobs, do they complement or inform each other? At what point does the creative impulse diverge between poetry and music?

They're of a piece, in one sense. I play Irish traditional music, and I feature on a CD with a jazz band called Lammas with Don Paterson playing guitar and I've worked with a sampling composer, John Wall, using sample speech, building up music from spoken voices. It's experimental with a small e. I'm as interested in that kind of music as I am in traditional music. I think it's the same impulse all round, in fact. The same satisfaction you get from the reel can be held in the mind's hand all at once – it's almost tactile. You internalize the sixteen beats and that's the ground on which you play the tune, and I feel the same is true of the poem. At the unconscious level, it's like a watch, as in 'your eyes are getting heavy', a hypnotist's watch, familiar from end-of-the-pier shows. This is why Plato threw poets out of the Republic, because the form reaches you below the conscious level. Prose is the language of doubt and circumspection, and verse is the hypnotist's watch. The struggle for poets is how to use the hypnotist's tools to wake up the reader.

Your place of birth, your ancestry and your current home would appear to give you access to three literary traditions. How distinct are those traditions and to which do you feel closest?

They're all very mixed up at this stage. Growing up in the Spanish-speaking neighbourhood of the South Bronx, my parents told me that I was not American but Irish. I remember they were very hurt when I would say to them, 'But I am American.' I always felt like an outsider and could never really get into American literary nationalism, which is very strong. People are constantly competing to be the 'New American Voice'. I was never concerned with being nationally anything, but with just writing the poem. I really don't see the point of all that. I think this particularly now that I'm living in Britain and when I look back on American literature, and particularly modernist poets like William Carlos Williams who were rabid Anglophobes, and hated everything about Britain, as did Pound after his success soured – he went off Britain completely. American literature has an enormous inferiority complex. William Carlos Williams hated Eliot: he always considered his emigration a great betrayal; he seemed to take it personally.

I think Frost said that Eliot abandoned America and never quite reached England.

I think Frost was wrong. History has shown us a thoroughly anglified Eliot adopted by the English, and a sanitized and canonized Pound adopted by the Americans. I've been looking at this. The New Formalists really brought it to a head. Some of these people are friends of mine and I'm willing to take any help that they're prepared to give me, but I have to say that I don't want to be a part of any movement: it's all PR – it boxes you in, and I don't like that. I hate manifestos, consciously saying: 'I write a certain way, and this is the way I'm going to write.' I think Larkin said it's fatal to decide what a good poem is, because you are honour-bound to write that poem instead of the poem you're meant to write. If I had to choose one positive attribute of the jumble of styles critics are pleased to call 'postmodern', it's the freedom and eclecticism that keeps writer and reader constantly alert.

To what extent have you ever considered yourself an Irish poet?

I was at Fordham University as an undergraduate and did a course using Kinsella's translation of the Táin. My first-year Eng. Lit. teacher there, Mary FitzGerald, introduced me to Heaney back in '74 and we all went to hear Robert Lowell read, so I got very into Heaney. I of course found Heaney a great poet, but I found Mahon even more liberating – that urbanity, the humour. It was so liberating to discover that you could do this, write beautiful, memorable language and yet still be funny and ironic. So I never pursued an Irish identity. I just sort of backed into it. I'm not interested in literary nationalism of any kind. What was it Pound said? Studying American poetry is like studying American chemistry, something like that. I may have been escaping American literary nationalism: the poetry that I was being force-fed at the time was poetry from people like Charles Olson, with great theories like a line was as long as the length of a breath – how much did that man smoke? Even a man with one lung could do better than that! But he was full of those vatic pronouncements – he copied that from Pound, I suppose, along with everything else. 'One perception must immediately follow and directly lead to a further perception' – that's not a direction for poetry. That's instructions for being awake!

You've gone on record as saying that Derek Mahon's collections of 1975, The Snow Party, *brought you back to poetry when you thought you were going to give it up.*

That sounds a bit odd when you consider that my first collection came out in 1988. But it brought me back, yes. It said, 'You can do this,' this is what great poetry does to a poet. It gives you something else to do; when you're getting tired it gives you somewhere else to go. But looking back into it, I never consciously pursued Irishness in any way. I was only ever Irish through my family, and most of my friends were Irish as a result of playing in a traditional band. And I happened to be turned on by poets like Mahon and Muldoon. Muldoon shows you a direction of modernism that's very different to American and British modernism: it's Joyce's modernism.

You were chosen as one of the New Generation poets. What was your involvement and what did you make of the whole promotion?

Here's what happened. I didn't know anything about this and then I got a phone call from my publisher asking was I forty yet. And I said, 'No,' and put the phone down. And then a week later, I got a phone call saying, 'Congratulations, you are a New Generation Poet,' which has a horrible sound. Occasionally, I'll do a reading and someone will insist on saying, 'Tonight we have Michael Donaghy who is a New Generation Poet,' and this grey-haired forty-three-year-old gets up on stage. It sounds awful, and it was. I hate to sound ungrateful, and I'm sure it did me some good, but there was almost nothing to it. Carol Ann Duffy, to her credit, refused to participate in most of it. I complained again and again to journalists, although no one quoted me. No one said there was anything wrong. if they said they'd chosen twenty poets who were all white males, there would have been outrage, but to chose twenty poets who were all under forty was considered a good thing. After that what happened was, they said, 'Keep October free – don't do any readings, you're going to have lots of readings.' In the end, I did far fewer readings than I would have done, getting them off my own bat. But really, the only people who remember it are poets who weren't included.

Can that kind of marketing impinge on the writing process?

No – I don't give a puff for being famous. I was talking to Kathleen Jamie about this at the time, about having people running up to you and saying, 'Will you do this – you'll be on the *television*.' It's very nice to have people buy your books, and that's what we all want, for people to read our work, but there's only so much you will do. The whole thing was an embarrassment. It sounds ungrateful saying all this, and sometimes it was nice to be in the same room as nineteen of my friends. I think it helped out some people whose work should be better known – I think it gave Don Paterson a push, and I think he certainly deserves it, he's a great poet. I think that Kathleen Jamie acknowledges that she needed the push, but I don't think that Simon Armitage or Glyn Maxwell needed any help.

Much of your new work since Errata *seems to concern your father. How has writing about your father affected your work, and has it made it more confessional?*

They say the page is a curtain and you never know who's on the other side. It is interesting for me to write about my father and it is interesting for me to write about myself, but I don't feel any commitment towards reality or towards the details of our relationship. There's a tremendous anxiety of, in Walter Jackson Bate's phrase, 'the burden of the past on the English poet'. There is the burden of one's contemporaries writing about one's fathers. I don't want to be on page 20 of the Faber *Anthology of Father Poems*. (I think there actually is going to be such an anthology.) All of this brings us into the realm of my personal life which I'm not interested in discussing. I haven't written that much about my father: I've written a poem called 'Caliban's Books', one called 'The Excuse' and another 'Not Knowing the Words' and I think that's it. Oh, and there was a poem called 'Letter' in the first book, which is a very young person's poem, a very naive poem: there seems to be something very artless about it. But I'm afraid it's one of those poems I've decided to include in my tiny selection in the Penguin *Modern Poets Selection*, because that's the poem about which my relatives come up to me and say, 'That's the only poem of yours I understand,' and I haven't got the heart to leave it out.

A poem like 'The Commission' in Errata *suggests an interest in longer narrative forms. Is this a direction in which you would like your work to move?*

Yes, it is. I've just broken a long stretch of not writing, and I feel excited about the possibilities of writing again. I've written a long, three-page thing that people will probably think is very confessional. Perhaps I've protected myself against that by making it a dramatic monologue. Obviously I'm very comfortable with the lyric form and the lyric impulse, but I'd like to move in more dramatic and narrative directions and use different rhetorical strategies. I enjoyed writing 'The Commission', and there's an experiment in that poem, in that, as you may have guessed, it's based around Benvenuto Cellini. I had an idea in mind of making him the metalsmith who fashioned the bird of gold enamelling that winds up singing for the Emperor in Yeats's poem, but the poem went off in its own direction – an exploration of rage – my rage and desire for revenge – compared with an artist's rage for order. There's also a formal experiment in that poem: I wanted to write a single dactylic line with visual breaks like free-verse line endings – a continuous rhythm from beginning to end, without a break.

Has the success of Shibboleth, *which won both the Whitbread Prize and the Geoffrey Faber Memorial Prize, put pressure on your subsequent works?*

Yes, it has. *Errata* is a better book, but it didn't win anything. Although it did get me a cheque in the middle of the night when I was financially in dire straits. Someone delivered a letter from America in the middle of the night that had gone to my old address. I heard it come through my letterbox just as I was walking down the stairs in a blind panic about money. I opened it up and it was a cheque for, well, a small fortune from the Ingram Merrill Foundation. It was almost the last thing that James Merrill did before he died, to send me a small fortune.

God bless him!

God bless him! But I thought that *Errata* should have received more attention – it was a better book than *Shibboleth*. *Shibboleth* was perhaps a little over-praised, and *Errata* suffered because of that. It happens to every poet though, after you publish a book, you go through a period where you think none of your current ideas live up to your last achievement. A part of you thinks, 'I've done it, what should I do now?' It took five years to write *Errata*, but my work didn't suffer, just the perception of my work, which is a very different thing. I remember on the way up to get the Geoffrey Faber Memorial Award in the Faber offices, I met D. J. Enright in the lift. After the Whitbread Prize, he was calling me 'Dear boy'. By the time I met him on the way up to get the Faber Award, he was asking me 'So, when will you be going home to America?'

Interview with Andy Brown, 1998

Does 'abstract' or 'experimental' really mean 'elitist'?

Yes. Not that there's anything especially wrong with that. But look at those sexy words used all too frequently to describe contemporary art and literature, 'experimental' and 'revolutionary'. The first is a metaphor filched from science – experimental art doesn't have a control group, doesn't collate and publish its findings. And 'revolutionary' properly describes a brick thrown at a police cordon, not a poem in *Parataxis*. Among the most cherished illusions of the avant-garde is the idea that bourgeois art consoles, pleases and mollifies with received notions of beauty, whereas avant-garde art shocks and challenges and doesn't seek to please. I'm always dismayed by this kind of self-delusion. The audience for avant-garde art is a middle-class audience that pays to be shocked, or bored or insulted, in much the same way that Mistress Wanda's clients pay to be horsewhipped. It's an audience that knows what it wants and is comfortable with its rituals and cliches. Whether it's a urinal on a pedestal in 1910 or a poem composed entirely of semi-colons in 1997 ('everything changes but the avant-garde', said Auden), the audience expects to retreat from a direct and complex experience of the craftsmanship, to ideas about art.

The most common of these ideas can be phrased as 'Justify your instinctive reaction that this is not a work of art.' In other words, the burden of proof is placed with the audience, where in former ages it belonged to the artist. Whatever the quality of your work, if it strikes the critical powers-that-be as 'anti-poetic', it is de facto worth talking about. Fine. I enjoy avant-garde work from Duchamp to Damien Hirst, to poets like Clark Coolidge, but let's not delude ourselves with the naive and sentimental notion that such art is 'progressive'. I'm angry about that pretence. Capitalism long ago defeated the avant-garde by accepting it as another style. Yet artists continue to present themselves as an offence to the establishment even as they accept fat cheques from the Saatchi Gallery or attend academic conferences on 'oppositional' poetries.

I feel very strongly that we have to be vigilant about naked emperors, otherwise mediocrities become cultural referents. Any random shape, crash of noise or verbal incomprehensibility can become comfortingly familiar – the perfect representation of itself – by answering its own echo or after-image in our unconscious. Say your dog pees on the carpet. Every day we see the stain and eventually we get used to it. Put that stain on a wall, track lit, in a gallery, run a debate on its merits in the Sunday supplements, refer to it archly in advertising – sooner or later it will become iconic. It will have cultural importance, because we all recognize it. It becomes a cultural referent and will provide all those bourgeois satisfactions that the avant-garde profess to despise. And all because no one stood up and said it was piss.

Is there any validity in the terms that are used to divide poetry up into 'schools', or are they just marketing devices?

Marketing devices. Either that, or terms used by academics to group poets into convenient geographical or historical chapter headings. Harriet Monroe of *Poetry* (Chicago) cautioned a reluctant Louis Zukovsky that he couldn't just collect good poems for an issue he was guest editing. 'You must have a movement. Give it a name,' she said – and Objectivism was born. Zukovsky was referred to Monroe by Pound who was, of course, the P. T. Barnum of his movement. I wonder how any serious poet can limit him or herself by declaring allegiance to a particular way of writing poetry. As Malcolm Bradbury said in *Eating People Is Wrong*: Sorry, no movement. All made up by the Literary Editor of the *Spectator*.

In what sense are poets working in the 'mainstream' and in the 'modernist experimental' traditions dealing with the same problems?

Aren't these terms a little too neat? Is John Ashbery mainstream? Paul Muldoon? Jorie Graham? They're all 'difficult' poets and they're all highly celebrated and be-medalled. 'Mainstream', like 'middlebrow', is more often than not a dismissive term used by avant-garde artists to describe more famous rivals. If 'mainstream' means 'accepted', then Language poetry, for example, is in the vanguard of the mainstream. It purports to challenge the means of production, but when the academic establishment turns its hungry eye on contemporary verse, it turns to the Language poets. In American universities they are discussed in seminars and anthologized by major publishers like Norton (their books produced in the same paper mills and factory as any other book). Of course, their poems would never be read by the men and women who work in those factories. Language poetry makes nothing happen.

Where is poetry heading? Is poetry that homogeneous an activity?

Substitute the word 'music' for 'poetry' in those two questions and you see the kind of assumptions made about poetry. Blues musicians on the South Side of Chicago, jazz pianists in London, fiddlers in West Clare, electro-acoustic composers in Rotterdam – we wouldn't dream of measuring them by the same standard, ranking them or telling them where we think 'music' is going. Poetry is *not* a homogeneous activity. And art *has no direction*. This is spatial illusion generated by early twentieth-century ideas about 'advancement' and 'progress'. If it's hard to see this now, it's because the illusion is augmented by the demands of consumerism. Our economy depends on the notion that things and ideas become obsolete and have to be replaced. Products of art and literature can be sold more effectively if they're marketed as 'new' so that newness acquires an all-pervasive fetish value. There was a lot of fuss made about the New Generation Poets (a public-relations exercise in which, to my shame, I participated). But very little of that fuss concerned the exclusion of poets over forty. We're on our guard against racism and sexism, but ageism is built into our economy.

Is poetry for the page, or are you more interested in the oral tradition / performance?

I'm *exclusively* interested in a poetry that takes its direction and rhythm – like all traditional poetry – from the voice. Concrete poetry doesn't interest me in the least. Most 'experiments' with typographical arrangements strike me as contemptibly silly. I've done innumerable readings in the past decade and I regard the aural performance of poetry an art form. I'm not a performance poet, but I've worked with performance poets and I respect some as poets and many as entertainers, but for me a rewarding poem has layers and requires of its reader maximum concentration and focus. If such a poem goes over well in performance – that's a bonus.

Charles Olson, that virtuoso of the typewriter, said that verse in rhyme, metre and stanzas was 'verse which print bred'. Olson was a fool. Memorizable form evolved according to the demands of the voice.

Are content and form working as one in your poetry, or do you see it working along different lines from such a traditional division?

I'm not sure there is a clear-cut 'traditional' division. Let me explain: on the simplest level, *form* functions for any poet as a kind of *scaffold* from which the poem can be constructed. Stravinsky maintained that only in art could one be freed by the imposition of more rules, perhaps because these rules limit the field of possibilities and escort us rapidly beyond the selection of tools and media to laying the first stone of the work itself. For the reader, on the other hand, the shared language of the poem functions as a *map* through the terrain of a new idea. Traditionally, narratives or arguments are parted into, for example, episodes in which three wishes are granted, or rhetorical points explored. Expressions like 'on the one hand . . .'

warn the listener to bracket the ensuing information and prepare for its antithesis '. . . and on the other . . .' exploiting reader or audience expectation.

But I'm more interested in the unconscious or subliminal effects of reading and writing in form. The effect of form on the reader is like the hypnotist's dangling fob watch, familiar from end-of-the-pier shows and B-movies ('Your eyes are getting heavy'). We are hypnotized or spellbound by form, because the traditional aural techniques of verse, the mnemonics of rhyme, metre and rhetorical schemes, are designed to fix the poem in the memory, to burn it in deeper than prose. But think of the unconscious effect of form on the poets themselves. This is the most interesting aspect of tradi-tional technique, and it represents the intervention of that presence – or sense of presence – poets used to call the muse. Any degree of difficulty in a form requires of the poet that s/he negotiate with the medium, and compromise what s/he originally 'spontaneously' intended to say. (So far so good, since one's spontaneous reaction is always more likely to be full of self-deception, prejudice and cliche.) That peculiar sensation, that the best image or line simply 'came to us', as if delivered by an unseen presence, comes from our own unconscious of course. The feeling of 'otherness' is explained by the fact that our self-perception is firmly rooted in our waking consciousness.

Have you collaborated with other writers or artists on any work recently? How has this developed your poetry?

I've made a poem / film with Miranda Pennell, *Habit*. The collabo-ration came out of my interest in the formal techniques of the cinema, the way our visual vocabulary exploded in a few decades to include focus pulls, slow pans, montage and cross-cuts, and the way this influenced the other arts. In fact, this proved to be a problem in making the film – twentieth-century poetry is so concrete, so image-heavy, that it's often a poor relation of film. I realized my task was to undercut or augment the images on screen with verbal rhythms. I also realized I could be abstract, because the film was providing the imagery. I've also collaborated with the *musique concrète* composer John Wall on a poem for voices using sampling techniques – this is more in the order of a piece of music using samples of speaking voices.

Interview with Nick Cobic, 2002

You first came to the UK in 1985. What made you want to come in the first place?

The food. Just kidding. I moved here to be near my girlfriend.

You decided to drop out from the judging panel for this year's Forward Prize. Why did that happen?

There were allegations of bias. A pretty absurd idea if you think about it carefully. If you are talking about the awarding of government contracts, for example, the word 'bias' is scandalous. But in something subjective like an arts prize you want the judges to be true to their tastes. That's what they're paid for. The suggestion that a poet judging the prize is going to favour his or her friend's book over one he or she knows to be superior strikes me as silly. Especially as there are five judges involved and the voting is confidential. But once the allegations of bias were made, my involvement was bound to come up because two of us on the panel are published by Picador, which is no surprise, and it could just as easily have been two poets published by Faber and Faber. After the allegations were made it suddenly became an issue. I dropped out so that the judges won't have to worry about accusations during the second part of judging.

What is the shortest way to success?

Always carry a spoon in case it rains soup.

What would be your advice to a non-established poet that wishes to be known?

Assassinate a public figure.

Does poetry come from the unconscious?

I'm not sure I believe in the unconscious. *The Interpretation of Dreams* was published in 1900 and as of today there's still no scientific evidence for the existence of the phenomenon as it's described by Freud or Jung. But of course I acknowledge the existence of the irrational, of subliminal urges, the places we go when we dream, the sudden insight, lateral thinking, etc. However, I believe the fully conscious mind engages all of the above.

Do you think that mistakes too make a poet?

It may indeed be a mistake to be a poet.

As well as being a poet, you are also a musician. Does music inspire your poetry? Does poetry inspire your music?

I've often been asked to explain the relationship between traditional music and my writing. There isn't one, really. I just happen to play the flute a bit and I've written a couple of poems exploring Irish traditions. But if pressed I'll concede there is a common root in orality. The music I play survives in an aural tradition, whether or not it may also be packaged as a product nowadays, its essential nature belongs to the free exchange of tunes among non-professional musicians who learned from their families and communities and who play for the love of playing, for each other and for dancers. Most of the musicians I know don't read music and they've picked up their vast repertoires of jigs and reels – hundreds of tunes and variations – by ear. And this is the original situation of verse. The mnemonic groove established by a traditional musical form like a reel or a blues or a raga is analogous to the traditional oral mnemonics of poetry. There's a great smiliarity between, say, a sonnet and a jig, as they both have a particular form and can consequently be held in the mind. Every sonnet is in one sense like every other sonnet and I think this is the original situation with verse. It is the information storage for pre-literate culture. It exists today because it reaches the part of our mind that prose can't reach.

To what extent can a translation change a poem and how much freedom should a translator have to stray from the original?

Frost remarked that 'Poetry is what is lost in translation', and what he means is the very subtle connotations that every word has cannot possibly be translated from one language to another, so the resonance between words and the music between words which matter so much to the poem cannot be translated. Poets throughout history have tried heroically to do this. Pound was the first to introduce the notion of versions. He would often work from a prose translation and turn it into a poem by Ezra Pound. If you call it a version you are entitled to stray as much as you like. If, however, you want to call it a translation, your duty is to communicate as much as possible and as closely as possible. In the end all translations are versions of the original.

How do you prepare for your poetry readings?

I don't sit down and memorize poems. By the time I finish a poem I usually have it memorized. I used to prepare for poetry readings by drinking as much as possible, because I was so nervous. I don't do that at all now. I guess I don't really prepare for readings at all. Sometimes I write a list of poems that I intend to read.

How will new technological inventions change poetry?

Here we come dangerously close to actually trying to give a definition of poetry. The word 'poetry' means a made thing and doesn't define anything. People generally take it as an art form of combining words. Beyond that everything is up for grabs. The more exact term is 'verse'. It exists today in relation to voice, body, speech, presence and memory. Some new forms of technology, like the Internet, are wonderful at distributing poetry. There are ways of playing games with words on the Internet and thus create your own poems. Personally I regard it as more of a game than an art form. The essential nature of verse will not change as it has been the same since prehistoric times.

It has been tried to use computers to write poems. No doubt, some day computers will be made to fall in love and have sex, so I guess they will write poems to each other as well.

Interview with John Stammers, 2003

You're not a prolific poet, are you? Only three collections in fifteen years. In fact, the word count of your interviews to date threatens to exceed that of your collected poems. Can you bear to once again 'tell us a bit about your background'?

It does seem perverse that the author of three skinny little books should be the subject of so many 'profiles'. I'm ambivalent about interviews for four reasons. First, I'm not the definitive authority on my work. In fact, I'm not at all sure I write my books. I feel it's more the case that my books get written through me. Second, I wind up making insufferably pretentious statements like that last one. Third, I like to think my work is still developing and I suspect that any attempt to 'explain' myself interferes with or limits that development. And finally, I'd like to be remembered for my poems, not my charming personality. I say this not because I'm an especially reticent or private individual – but because my work has a life of its own and, if it works, it's as much 'about' the reader's life as about mine. But it seems impossible to confine a discussion of this nature to matters of technique.

So, with that off my chest I'll return to your question. I was born in the South Bronx, New York, in 1954. My parents had emigrated from Ireland after the war and both took jobs at the Statler Hilton hotel in Manhattan – my mother, a Kerry woman, working as a maid and my father, from Belfast, in the boiler room. They married, had two children, and then we moved back to Ireland for a bit because my father had hopes of finding work back in Belfast. They always regarded themselves as Irish-in-exile so this was to be their triumphant return home. But the work never materialized, so we returned, broke, to the Bronx, where my father eventually got work in a factory that made printing presses. My most enduring memories of my childhood are related to the violence of that neighbourhood – horrific street violence – and that I suppose, together with a delirious histrionic experience of Catholicism, tends to crop up in my work in one guise or another. I could say it was a hard life, and perhaps I should, but my childhood friends would laugh to hear me putting on 'the poor mouth'. After relating these details in several interviews my story is beginning to sound like an over-dramatized application for marginality status, the cliché sob-story of the working-class writer. In fact, I grew up in one of the wealthiest cities in the world, and our hardship differed substantially from that of our non-white neighbours in that we could realistically hope to escape our situation. And, of course, I did.

And you moved to Britain. Why?

I moved to London in 1985 in pursuit of a beautiful and talented Englishwoman I met in Chicago. We'd lived in Chicago together for a time and when her visa expired I followed her home. Twenty years on, I'm finally off the dole, Maddy and I are still together – just got married in fact – and we have a son, Ruairi.

The O'Ryan's Belt sequence acknowledges your Irishness. Why especially did you want to write that?

Let's leave aside for the moment the question of whether I sought to 'acknowledge my Irishness' and what that might mean. I've said elsewhere that my origins are Irish Catholic and proletarian, and those are not elective affinities. You never fully escape those influences no matter how hard you try. But I hasten to add that the accidents of my bloodlines and my interest in traditional music are not elements of a securely autobiographical poetry. They're just factors I've sometimes exploited on my way to exploring dimensions of tradition and culture. I've only alluded to Irish music and Irishness in a handful of poems in order to approach issues of orality, sentimentality, nationality and memory. I've used other musics: Mozart, Purcell, Curtis Mayfield and John Cage crop up, 'Footage from the Interior' draws on African log drumming, 'Down' on the blues, in 'Theodora Theodora' I use rembetika, in 'The Palm' it's jazz and in 'Ramon Fernandez' I allude to partisan songs of the Spanish Civil War. But I knew that once I broached the matter of Irishness or Irish folk music I'd be typecast as 'the Irish American musician poet' – so I delayed publishing those poems until after my first collection.

I've often been asked to expand on the relationship between traditional music and my writing. There isn't one, really. My parents sang and played the odd tune, I just happen to play the flute a bit myself, and I've written a couple of poems exploring Irish traditions. But if pressed I'll concede there's a common root in orality; the music I play survives in an oral/aural tradition, whether or not it may also be packaged as a product nowadays, its essential nature resides in the free exchange of tunes among non-professional musicians who learned from their families and communities, and who play for the love of playing, for each other, and for dancers. Most of the musicians I know don't read music and they've picked up their vast repertoires of jigs and reels – hundreds of tunes and variations – by ear. And this is the original situation of verse. The mnemonic groove established by a traditional musical form like a reel or a blues is analogous to the traditional oral mnemonics of poetry.

And what about these Hispanic references in your work – old childhood friends, Latin American music, etc.?

As I said earlier, my childhood environment crops up in my work in one guise or another – but never in a straightforward autobiographical way. The South Bronx at that time was a very mixed community of Puerto Ricans, Panamanians, Haitians and African-Americans, together with a dwindling older population of Irish and Italians, and the atmosphere was often electric with racial tension. But in the schools I attended, where the groups *had* to mix, it was language rather than skin colour that divided us, and it took some time for the English and Spanish speakers to trust and befriend one another. Outside of school the streets fell more and more under the control of increasingly dangerous gangs. One group was led by two very colourful brothers, Caesar and Hector, whom I both admired and feared. I recognize this ambivalence in Borges's clearly awestruck descriptions of the knife-fighters of his Buenos Aires childhood, and I suppose the South Bronx is my 'South Side'.

What about your education? Often, poets from working-class backgrounds reject the shibboleths of 'highbrow' culture. But your work is self-consciously literary in that there's an intertextual agenda for most of the poems. Entire lines from Pound and Pope and Marvell turn up from time to time.

My father left school at fourteen but he was an autodidact with a broad range of passions which included mysticism and machinery. My early interest in modern poetry began with two or three anthologies he purchased in a used bookshop on the Lower East Side. I think they were edited by Oscar Williams. He never got around to reading them, but I did. Before Donald Allen's *The New American Poetry* many US poetry anthologies featured British and Irish as well as American poetry, and as a boy I was intoxicated by the music in Hopkins and Dylan Thomas. Later I attended Fordham University in the Bronx and came under the tutelage of the Jesuits and the spell of David Jones. I devoured the *Anathemata* and wrote about the Neo-Thomist aspect of his poetics. I've only recently realized how much I still owe to my immersion in Jones and Maritain – their underlying aesthetic, that is, not Jones's poem. I also became an avid Poundian, having swallowed whole the mystique promoted by works like Hugh Kenner's *The Pound Era*, a delusion I suffered for several years. I still read and admire much in Pound, of course, but I'm no longer a member of the cult.

Around this time, 1974 I think, I enrolled on a course in twentieth-century Anglo-Irish literature taught by a tremendously enthusiastic young woman, Mary FitzGerald. The course was entirely Joyce and Beckett, but she also introduced us to a contemporary Irish poetry scene which I found more exciting than the mostly dull stuff on the reading list for the contemporary American poetry course. She invited Heaney to come and read at Fordham. He was extremely generous to our little circle of undergraduate English majors and we all went on an expedition to hear Robert Lowell read in Manhattan. She also introduced me to Derek Mahon, whose work, the polar opposite of Pound's, or indeed Jones's high Modernism, I found very seductive. It was a revelation to encounter this singing line, this wit, this panache, this performed personality, after the vast solemn impersonal footnoted systems of the Modernist long poem. I imagine Mahon provided the same kind of enabling influence that you say you found in the work of Frank O'Hara, John. Earlier you suggested that some of my poems represent an impulse to 'acknowledge my Irishness'. If I ever had that impulse it was then, in my early twenties.

In 1977 I went west to the University of Chicago where I pursued and abandoned a PhD. I was lucky to encounter some inspiring teachers there as well: among them, James Chandler, W. J. T. Mitchell, and Robert Von Hallberg, who introduced me to the work of Elizabeth Bishop and James Merrill. Chicago was in transition in the late seventies. The last remaining dinosaurs of the 'Chicago School' were being shouldered aside by the rise of a more aggressive species, the new literary theory. Derrida came to lecture and de Man offered a seminar. Now – you may have noticed – I have a problem with authority, and this was authority writ large. I also have a problem with deadlines, and I couldn't capitulate to either the zeitgeist or the timetable. I allowed myself to be sidetracked into playing Irish music and leading a dissolute lifestyle. I also drifted into editing the poetry section of a magazine called the *Chicago Review* and despite, or because of, encountering reams of terrible poetry week after week, I started writing in earnest what I then took to be *good* poetry. Looking back now, much of it was execrable. I went through an Ashbery phase, and wrote what amounted to a book-length collection of sub-Ashbery smartass surrealist verse. It didn't take very long, and I've never recycled a single phrase of it. I changed tack, accumulated a very different batch of poems, and finally I published a chapbook, *Slivers*, which forms the basis of the collection I later published in Britain as *Shibboleth*.

I suppose the relative frequency of literary allusion in my earlier work is a natural effect of writing poetry in an academic environment. It probably doesn't help to introduce the semiotic notion of intertextuality, but my experience of the transmission and performance of Irish music might be worth mentioning again in this context. In such an aural/oral tradition you don't strive for novelty, and the only 'personal expression' you achieve comes as a result of subordinating your personality to the tradition – the tune must play through you. I remember reading Eliot's 'Tradition and the Individual Talent' at the time and thinking it especially relevant to the Irish folk tradition: 'No poet, no artist of any art, has his complete meaning alone. His significance, his appreciation is the appreciation of his relation to the dead poets and artists . . . what happens when a new work of art is created is something that happens simultaneously to all the works of art which preceded it.'

Around 1980 I was working as a part-time librarian in the Joseph Regenstein Library and using its vast resources I started doing independent research on a genre I termed 'mathetic satire' which included works as varied as [Bruno's] *De Immenso*, the *Scienza Nuova*, the *Biographia Literaria*, *A Vision* and *Finnegans Wake* (in relation to its accompanying critical anthology, the *Exagmination*) – texts that mix discursive prose with verse or in other ways foreground the *mise en page* – the paraphernalia of footnotes, marginalia and diagrams – paratextuality, if you'll forgive a theoretical buzzword – to ironic effect. I suppose it all goes back to my undergraduate interest in David Jones, and to his mentor Eric Gill's concern with the physical nature of the book.

Your monograph Wallflowers, *'a lecture on poetry with misplaced notes and additional heckling', makes liberal use of these effects. Did it develop from this idea?*

Yes. *Wallflowers* begins, as the title might suggest, with a meditation on dance, which R. G. Collingwood called 'the mother of language'. We tend to 'grasp' abstract ideas in physical metaphors – metaphors of gesture or bodily movement through space. We may record a higher status to abstract thought, but all abstraction is a system of concrete metaphors unanchored from their roots in the physical world. Even as basic an abstraction as the verb 'to be' is rooted in the Sanskrit *bhu*, 'to grow', whereas 'am' and 'is' share a root with the Sanskrit *asmi*, 'to breathe'. Consider the way we visualize our own consciousness to ourselves – a roomy mental arena, which we usually locate behind the eyes, though other cultures have placed it in the guts or the heart. But this is just another spatial illusion.

It's the same with our notions of time. We picture ourselves moving, or being moved, forward through time whereas the Greeks saw themselves as rooted solidly in the earth, with time flowing from behind bringing the future past them and revealing the effects of past action – thus we can 'see', which is to say remember, the past 'before' us, but not the future coming up from the rear. In Mandarin, on the other hand, the future is conceived as welling up from the ground. Our 'progressive' spatial metaphor for time shores up a great many twentieth-century ideas which have proved detrimental to society and the environment. As far as the arts are concerned, the absurdities are striking. For example, if Mozart himself returned and wrote a sequel to *Cosi Fan Tutti* in the same style, he would necessarily, according to the 'developmental' view, be making inferior music, or acting in bad faith, because he wouldn't be addressing the modern aesthetic and 'building on the advances' of his immediate predecessors. Once 'ahead of his time', he would now be 'moving backward' instead of 'forward'. And the same would hold for any artist we might hazard to call great and, of course, for anyone composing in as 'backward' an idiom as visual representation, tonality, or narrative.

In my work back in Chicago I traced the effects of illusions implicit in diagrams of abstract notions of mind and the creative process in order to identify a distinct genre in which diagrams are used ironically to challenge these illusions. In *Wallflowers* I applied some of these same ideas to poetry and considered the printed poem as a diagram of the interaction of poet and audience.

I should explain that by 'diagram' I mean a schematic picture. We all agree, after Gombrich, that pictures are highly conventional and often perpetuate illusions, but diagrams often represent processes rather than objects and the illusions are more insidious because the conventions can't be checked against a stable visible subject. A great many suspect ideas – misrepresentations of Freud or Darwin or quantum physics, for example – persist because they've been 'visualized' in diagrams. You mentioned intertextuality – well, Kristeva diagrams this notion in terms of horizontal and vertical axes. And think of Lacan's ill-advised recourse to topology.

Earlier you mentioned Eliot, the most allusive of poets, and I note that your poem 'The Drop' takes an Eliot poem as a model. Sorry to keep on with this issue of intertextuality, but what role does allusion play in your work?

So you've spotted 'Journey of the Magi' behind my *film noir* version. That poem was the result of an exercise in allusive form in which I moved away gradually from the original to an entirely new poem. Of course, Eliot himself drew heavily and openly on such methods. For example, his poem begins with five lines in quotation marks derived from a sermon delivered in 1622 by Bishop Launcelot Andrewes. Pound is another strong presence in the poem, particularly the 'Exile's Letter'. In Pound's poem, there's an ageing narrator, far from home and friends, who recalls with regret past meetings and past journeys, one of them 'hard going, over roads twisted like sheep's guts', another involving an idyllic sojourn in 'a valley of a thousand flowers'. Both of which wind up utterly transformed in Eliot's and finally in my poem. Also, you'll have found the formal architecture of 'The Drop', its syntax and temporal shifts, is a tracing of 'Journey of the Magi'. So in setting out to re-write Eliot's poem into something of my own, I'm acknowledging several nested literary debts.

An obvious question now: you're an Irish-American poet much celebrated in Britain but virtually unknown in America. How would you describe your transition from an American to a British poetry culture and how would you describe the difference between those two cultures?

There's quite a difference. I arrived in Britain in 1985 and received a contract for *Shibboleth* with OUP the same year, having published only one poem in a little magazine. As you can imagine, I was regarded as something of an *arriviste*. One thing that struck me immediately about British poetry upon my arrival was its sheer visibility, its contract with a middle-class 'common reader'. You can imagine my culture shock arriving from eighties America, where literary poetry was confined to an academic subculture, and finding there really existed a significant population of literate individuals who took poetry seriously. Entire programmes of poetry were broadcast on the radio; poetry was regularly reviewed in the broadsheets; a poetry collection had just won the country's biggest literary prize; the appointment of the Poet Laureate was headline news! Brodsky maintained that the role of poetry in society depends upon the audience, not the poet. And Britain had, and still has, that audience – an audience which has kept poetry at the heart of British literary culture: think of the popularity of Byron and Tennyson, or in this past century think of Masefield's Collected selling 80,000 copies in its first print run, or think of the poets of the Great War and what they continue to signify in British culture. Just this morning [Jan 9th, 2003] as I answer your question, a poem by the Poet Laureate made *front-page news* in the broadsheets! It's not an everyday occurrence – the poem was deemed newsworthy because it was critical of US-led policy on Iraq – but the fact that a thirty-word quatrain made the headlines says a good deal about the enduring position of poetry in British culture. I suppose it's the middle-class manifestation of a surviving native predisposition to verse evident in such near extinct populist forms as Cockney patter verse and Lancastrian recitations, a tradition that exists today alongside more recent imports like dub poetry and Urdu recitation.

It seems to me that American poets and critics take a dim view of contemporary British poetry if they are at all aware of its existence. When they write about poetry's contact with the non-academic British public it's usually with contempt, stereotyping the British common reader as a kind of sentimental philistine. But in my experience this reader expects to be challenged, not mollified, though he or she remains free and uncowed by academic canon formation.

So are you an American or British or Irish poet?

I'm afraid the question has no meaning for me, though it seems to be of great concern to anthologists or journalists who feel the need to classify me. I've only rarely been mistaken for an Irish poet – the American Conference On Irish Studies once paid my way over to read in Wisconsin and I think they were disappointed when I arrived and they heard my accent. I read widely in all English-language poetries, my poetry is addressed to anyone who can read it, and I have no interest in promoting a particular national identity for myself as a poet. My friend Ian Duhig quotes Hugh of St Victor in this regard – 'The man who loves his homeland is a beginner, he to whom every soil is as his own is strong, but he is perfect for whom the entire world is a foreign country.' When I sit down to breakfast, however, I'm an imperfect Irish-American long-time resident of the cosmopolitan North London Borough of Haringey. But I'm also aware my cosy attitude is a middle-class luxury Haringey's hundreds of Kurdish and Somali refugees can't afford.

And who are some of the British poets you found important in your development? I mean twentieth-century poets.

How much space do we have? Apart from those I've already mentioned in this interview, W. S. Graham and Robert Graves. Among living poets, I'd like to acknowledge the tutelary presences of Roy Fisher and the Australian-born Peter Porter. I don't believe either of them have ever had much influence on my practice, but I've long admired their work and their integrity.

But you know, we've hardly mentioned the relationship of post-war British and *Irish* poetry and the intercourse of these two contemporary scenes. I cited Heaney and Mahon as personal influences earlier, and I should have mentioned Michael Longley. But Paul Muldoon, emerging from the subsequent generation of Northern Irish poets, opened new ground for an astonishing number of my British contemporaries, whether they'll admit it or not. He's been hugely significant. I'd also like to include Ciaran Carson and Eiléan Ni Chuilleanáin in this roster, not because they'd been overwhelmingly influential on this island, but because they're marvellous poets and deserve mention.

Would you care to expand on those British contemporaries you mention? You were part of the 'New Generation' movement of the early nineties, which included Carol Anne Duffy, Simon Armitage, Glyn Maxwell, Don Paterson, Michael Hofmann and Lavinia Greenlaw. Do you feel you share a set of values with this group?

Well, first of all, the 'New Generation' wasn't a movement. It was a marketing campaign devised by Peter Forbes, the then editor of *Poetry Review*, and by the publishers to promote their poetry lists. Twenty poets under forty were chosen by a panel of established 'literary' poets and editors, but the publicity was left to a public-relations firm called Colman-Getty, who represented us to the media as – pardon my shudder – 'the new rock and roll'. At the time the promotion was rightly criticized for failing to include any Afro-Caribbean poets, but no one seemed to think there was anything at all wrong with excluding *as a matter of policy* poets over the age of forty. That's what happens when you link literary taste with consumerism. Of course it was all horribly embarrassing and horribly successful. The public bought our books, public interest in poetry increased for a time, and a few younger British poets have recently told me it was the 'New Gen' coverage that first got them interested in poetry. So I suppose it wasn't all bad.

In regard to your second question, I don't want to fall into the trap of naming my 'top 10 poets'. As well you know, John,

The Shape of the Dance

contemporary British poetry is astoundingly diverse. Identify any
tendency or school or clique within it and you'll find poets who
strive for excellence and poets who churn out counterfeit goods. But
yes, I respect the poets you mention and I suppose I must share *some*
of their political and artistic values.

*Donald Davie said of your earlier work 'formal verse is seldom so
wiry'. How important is this formal sense of line for you? Of metre?
It certainly seems out of place emerging from the milieu of seventies
American poetry.*

Well, you could say it was a perfectly predictable reaction to decades
of American Post-Beat orthodoxy. After all, I belong to the same
generation as most of the poets associated with 'New Formalism'
though I think I differ from some New Formalists in my particular
approach to form and tradition. Yes, I've engaged with traditional
techniques, but for me technique is only important as a means to
serendipity and – a weary phrase – 'lateral thinking'. I'm interested
in negotiating with resistant forms because negotiation leads to
discovery. I've said elsewhere that if writing poems were merely a
matter of bulldozing ahead with what you'd already made up your
mind to say I'd have long ago given it up for something more
dignified. Ashbery once said that he's used the rules of the sestina
'as a probing tool rather than as a form in the traditional sense . . .
rather like riding downhill on a bicycle and having the pedals
push your feet. I wanted my feet pushed into places they wouldn't
normally have taken.' That's a good way to put it, but he's wrong
about tradition because what he describes is *precisely* a function of
'form in the traditional sense' – that serendipity provided by negoti-
ation with a resistant medium. The obstacles provided by tradition,
if taken seriously, provide probing tools as challenging as the
lipograms and palindromes used by Oulipo writers. The difference
is that poetry in traditional forms resonates with all the other poetry
attuned to that frequency down the millennia.

As for the milieu you mention, there were several competing
poetries in seventies America. The one I found most oppressive was

180

the new plain-style academic verse coming out of the burgeoning creative-writing departments, which was exactly the opposite of fifties academic verse; not formal, impersonal, intellectual and allusive, but formally enervated, autobiographical, anecdotal and heavily reliant on a paratactic minimalist syntax – 'plain American which cats and dogs can read!' I found these skinny little collections of simple declarative sentences less interesting than the hypotactic structures in good prose. I suppose it came of teaching 'The Red Wheelbarrow' to a generation of high school students. Through the sixties and early seventies this mode of poetry was still linked to the counterculture. It's astonishing how these poets retained their mystique of the radical and marginal even as they became heads of writing programmes and their poetry became the offical MFA style. The Beat movement was elected to the canon of American literature. To give you some idea, *Howl* was published the year I was born, but twenty years later when I sat my Graduate Record Exam, the first question related to that poem. One could now fail an exam on Ginsberg.

I was also reacting to various theories of 'projective' verse or the 'variable foot' which I regarded as sophistry – and that's understating the matter considerably. I was after concinnity and intricacy and something like the musical tension proposed by Frost when he speaks of 'getting cadences by skilfully breaking the sounds of sense with all their irregularity of accent across the regular beat of the meter'. I think that's what Davie meant by 'wiry'. *Every* sound in a line, every syllable, every phoneme, has the potential to alter the course of the poem. Any sounds admitted to a line without maximum consideration would be, to extend Davie's metaphor, 'flab'.

I expect this has something to do with the insects. An infestation of mechanical bugs seems to have grown through your three books – in 'The Commission' Cellini makes a 'spindly gold locust' for the Pope, in 'Celibates' a sideshow freak specializes in making 'clockwork crickets' which also turn up in the Arctic in 'True'. In 'Interviews' Marcel Duchamp fashions a miniature animated machine from watch parts. And 'Quease' ends with a rather terrifying 'noisy wind-up spider cut from tin'. Is the mechanical insect a metaphor for a Donaghy poem?

Well, I don't really like reducing my poems by explanation. It's like a comic explaining a joke or a lover analysing a kiss. But sure, that's certainly one tenor I had in mind. I originally intended to end 'The Commission' with the Cellini character starting on his next project, the mechanical nightingale for Yeats's drowsy Emperor. But as the poem itself achieved autonomy through its form (in that case a single unbroken dactylic rhythm from start to finish with free verse line breaks) it decided its own ending. It's strange you should ask this question now. I'm currently engaged in a collaborative project with the Cybernetics Department at Reading University involving poetry and artificial intelligence. Just yesterday I visited their labs and encountered real autonomous mechanical insects and it was as though they'd just skittered out of my dreams. In a way, a poem is an artificial intelligence, not just 'a machine made out of words' but, as Don Paterson says, 'a machine for remembering itself'. I've noticed that any inanimate object of our concerted protracted attention appears to come alive and return that attention. This is especially true of works of art – think of Rilke's 'Archaic Torso of Apollo' – and it probably lies behind Romantic notions of organic form.

And in 'Machines' you say 'the machinery of grace is always simple'. I notice a preoccupation with mechanism of form and the 'ghost in the machine'.

Sure. But there's nothing new in that. Montale and W. C. Williams both likened poems to machines. Like them, I'm interested in simple and elegant works of linguistic engineering.

I know you admire many contemporary American poets – you've been a keen advocate of C. K. Williams and August Kleinzhaler, for example. But in several interviews you've acknowledged a special debt to the fifties generation of American formalists. Specifically, you've mentioned Richard Wilbur, Anthony Hecht, James Merrill, Donald Justice and Elizabeth Bishop. Are you announcing a particular allegiance to this tradition?

Well, I *do* hold these poets in the very highest regard. But I don't see this as a matter of 'allegiance' or 'loyalty'. It's not football, you know. And I don't believe in neatly binary oppositional accounts of literary history. Unfortunately, most historians of twentieth-century poetry do. The group you mention suffers from an image problem, in the public relations sense, because, as far as most of the authorities I've encountered are concerned, they lost the Anthology Wars to the poets of Donald Hall's *The New American Poetry* and, as usual, the victors have dictated their version of events. Hugh Kenner, James Breslin and so many other official accounts of post-war American poetry are terribly partisan and depend on using this group as an Aunt Sally – the 'tranquillized fifties', though I notice that in recent years they've been forced to find ways to admit Bishop into the canon, and nowadays they appear to be a little embarrassed by Olson.

I believe a lot of this is related to that venerable Anglophobic strain in American letters. A subplot of the grand metanarrative of monolineal 'cultural progress' might be entitled 'The Obsolescence of Britain'. In my view, these fifties east-coast formalists are disparaged because they represent the influence of Auden. In the fifties, remember, Auden's influence on American poetry was enormous. Bishop said that throughout the thirties and forties east-coast American poets read Auden constantly: 'We hurried to see his latest poem or book, and either wrote as much like him as possible, or tried hard not to.' He appeared at a point when the cultural autism of modernist hermeticism had run its course and he acted as a model for poets who wanted to return to poetry its public role without losing the imaginative adventurousness of modernism. And just as poets like Bishop and Hecht borrowed from Auden, Frost borrowed from Edward Thomas. It's clear that for poets loyal to the Pound/Williams line, this commerce with the English tradition represented a betrayal of the revolution, a pollution of American 'cultural purity'. So after the publication of Hall's anthology, Britain ceased to exist for many American poets. Even today, few American poets can name more than three or four of their British contemporaries. There's a kind of intellectual border mapped by market forces and nationalism, defended by the avant guard dogs.

You anticipate my next question. You have been a fierce critic of a certain tendency of the avant-garde to regard itself as cutting edge.

You make me sound so negative! This is a rather tedious issue because it appears to address important political issues but ultimately it's all a squalid little power struggle. It's generally agreed that 'poetry' has something to do with a special use of words but beyond that the term is up for grabs, and its etymology – *poesis*, 'making' – isn't much help narrowing the field. 'Poetry' appears to be whatever the accredited cultural arbiters of the day say it is; prayer, rap, limericks, tortured confessional free verse, song lyrics, sestinas, Zen koans, ironic *vers de société* and randomly chosen sentence fragments read backwards have all been classified or declassified as 'poetry', and everywhere we find poets and critics willing to offer their conflicting definitions or claim to know it when they see it. It's true I've been critical of a certain tendency that specializes in such definitions. But my criticism is directed at the attitude, not at the poetry. Discussions on either side of this conflict are marked by abusive caricature and simplification, but I'll try to keep this brief and fair.

You just used the expression 'cutting edge', a leaden cliché of advertising copy. Like 'avant-garde', 'innovation' and 'experimental' these are metaphors from science, technology and the military that survive because they serve the dynamics of marketing. There's a sexy cultural aura about a term like 'avant-garde', whether it's advertising poetry or a new perfume. The ferocity you mention registered my anger at the political dishonesty of a specific tendency in postmodernism – let's call it 'fundamentalist postmodern' – a tendency that's extremely hostile toward any poetry that's not aligned, with its offical programme. One of the most ardent American apologists for this tendency, Marjorie Perloff, has gone on record saying that what Robert Pinsky and Louise Glück do 'isn't poetry'. She cites Gertrude Stein as her authority here. These poets usually write in sentences which appear to proceed from a speaking subject, and, as Stein said of Hemingway, 'remarks are not literature'. The arts, like any other human activity, are subject to anthropological law, to tribal conflict, and it's worth noting that the names many indigenous peoples give themselves translate as 'human beings'. So in poetry you often see breakaway tribes claiming exclusive right to the name of poet. We're all familiar with the stereotype bourgeois philistine confidently pronouncing that the blank canvas or junk sculpture 'isn't art', but nowadays we're just likely to find the same priggish attitude struck by academic critics like Perloff.

In the States, of course, this tendency became organized in the early seventies as the Language movement, who styled themselves as the true heirs of experimental modernists like Stein. For years this group denied that they wanted to be recognized by what they called 'the marketplace of the culture industry' even as they struggled to elbow their way toward the centre of the academic marketplace through self-promotion and networking, playing the mavericks but apeing the very structures they still pretend to critique by means of these very bourgeois skills. And now they're very much at that centre, every bit as complacent and established as the 'official verse culture' they dismiss, publishing books with Harvard, Chicago, Princeton, Cambridge, Oxford and Norton, accredited cultural arbiters with the power to flunk students and dictate their patent definition of 'poetry'. And, most embarrassingly, they continue to style themselves 'underground', 'revolutionary' and 'marginal'. Charles Bernstein, the godfather of the movement, is now David Gray Professor of Poetry and Letters at Buffalo, a founding member of the Poetics Program and an associate member of the Comparative Literature Program. A couple of years ago he appeared doing a celebrity comic turn on US national television advertising the Yellow Pages at Rose Bowl half-time. How underground is that?

The attitude has become institutionalized. A considerable share of today's American creative-writing students are now writing not the poetic diction of the MFA free verse lyric, but theoretical discourse riddled with what you might call 'poetics diction'. This consists of some of the dullest sciolism in the history of prose, a standardized academic jargon and rhetoric, the dutiful rehearsal of received theory, and the deliberate misrepresentation of anything challenging or rejecting academic postmodernism as 'outmoded', 'unproblematic', sentimental or egotistical. It routinely caricatures the 'mainstream', lyric poem as the product of a Romantic conception of the self as a coherent entity, the lyric 'I' informed by experience, whereas the postmodern sensibility supposedly 'explodes the authoritative coherence of the self' or rather, assumes it's already exploded and doesn't have to do any risky munitions work. In fact, the 'self' in much contemporary verse outside the offical postmodern pale has been anything but 'unproblematic' and coherent.

The poetry I value makes use of the various musics, forms and narrative structures that are natural to our speech, however unusually they might manifest themselves. It also acknowledges the primacy of linguistic sense – even if that sense is hidden, or strange, or up for subversion. Most especially, we can read in the orientation of its spirit a particular relationship with the literal or imaginative truth. So it embodies the fact that poems are written by people, and their desire to communicate the truth – the deepest truth of which they have an inkling – at the sophisticated limit of their comprehensible speech. (By the way, this is why we have to safeguard the literary study of such poetry, since it is exclusively concerned with poetry's success or failure in its own terms – which necessarily include sense.) It is writing on the side of humanity, as this is how we, as human beings, speak, think and, by extension, live.

I suppose this raises the question of heteronymity. Your sequence 'Seven Poems From The Welsh' is presented as the work of a thirteenth-century Welsh poet – did you intend this as a literary hoax? Or is it a postmodern strategy?

Neither. I wrote 'Seven Poems' partly to try my hand at the *englyn*, a traditional form in Welsh poetry. It only seemed like a hoax because several readers and reviewers ignored my clear indications that Sion ap Brydydd was a 'mythical Welsh poet'. I can only suppose that they misread this as 'mystical'. In fact, several reviewers of my first book praised the 'accuracy' of the translations. Here's an amazing story – about two years ago I was at a party given by some of the parents at my son's school – far outside the literary perimeter – but somehow the conversation turned to art. I made some remark to the effect that great art took a long time, at which point a woman disagreed, chiming in with a story about an ancient poet who'd composed his best work the night before his execution and who'd composed an extremely complicated poem about the inside of an egg. It slowly dawned on me that this was my own Sion ap Brydydd and that eighteen years after I imagined him he'd developed a life of his own and passed into legend. I hesitated before telling her I'd made it all up, and when I did I'm not at all sure she believed me.

I suspect that some of the introductory epigraphs to your poems are authored by you. But creations like Sion ap Brydydd and his translator seem to belong to an earlier stage of your career. Have you now abandoned this heteronymic strategy?

I could say I use three or four identities and they all go by the name of 'Michael Donaghy'. In 1988 I published what you might call 'procedural' poems in the States under another name. I don't intend to reveal that name because my purpose in writing the poems was to explore an identity and a style, not to expose or humiliate editors. It's more difficult here in Britain because many UK journals that style themselves 'innovative' won't accept unsolicited submissions. But I'm afraid I'm more a Zelig than a Pessoa.

I am guilty of one act of deliberate disinformation, though. When I was at university I attended a few meetings of the Jung Foundation and during a question and answer session after a lecture I referred to a North African Gnostic belief that physical beings are

3D hieroglyphics in an infinite text continually being written by God. Someone must have been taking notes because some months later I found this fabrication reported as fact in one of their publications. It was irresponsible of me, I know, to take advantage of their trust. But it wasn't intended maliciously. It was more like 'memetic engineering' or hacking into reality, or like Borges's story 'Tlön, Uqbar, Orbis Tertius' in which a secret society conspires to forge entries about an imaginary realm in editions of an encyclopedia. But I'm sure it all boils down to neurosis. I've found the Internet a real temptation in this regard, and I've created umpteen Internet identities – all perfectly harmless, I hasten to add.

You do have a broader range of 'styles' than most of your contemporaries. It's unusual to see surreal prose poems like 'Where is it written that I must end here' or 'Alas Alice' alongside formal metaphysical poems, apparently confessional lyrics, and dramatic monologues all in quick succession in one volume.

Yes, my entry in the *Oxford Companion to Twentieth-Century Poetry* reads 'a poet who tries on so many suits is in danger of looking like a coat hanger'. When I first began sending my work out to magazines I'd get 'encouraging' rejections from American editors who found my work promising but 'affected', who felt I hadn't 'found my natural voice'. I've always distrusted that phrase. It sounds a little like finding a corporate image to increase consumer recognition.

But surely poetry is a person speaking, albeit in a special mode, so doing so in your own voice (untrammelled by convention or reserve) is something to aspire to, no?

No. Obviously words printed on a page are not 'a person speaking'. But if I should choose to exploit that illusion, why should the identifiable style of my 'voice' be deemed more authentic than yours? Or one of many voices I may have synthesized out of my reading and experience? And by the way, once you've identified your signature or voice or style, doesn't it then become another mask? Our word 'person' derives from the Greek for mask. Now you may believe that mask, or the mask you see every morning in the mirror, is the real you, but who holds that belief, who's looking through the eyes of that mask? No, the conscious use of a persona is not an index of 'reserve'. And Lear's grief is shattering whether or not we think we're getting the 'real' Will Shakespeare.

But doesn't this sound just a little like postmodernism? Language poets say that their work 'denies the centrality of the individual artist', and Lyn Hejinian says that 'the "personal" is already a plural condition . . . One can look for it and already one is not oneself, one is several, incomplete, and subject to dispersal.'

Sure, and I hear there's no Santa Claus either. Look, we all *know* the constructed self is a complex problem. There's no more commonplace idea in contemporary thought. And every poet wrestles with this issue in his or her unique way. The poets you mention are very vocal about challenging the 'bourgeois monad of the lyric "I"' but just try spelling their names wrong, or plagiarizing their manifestos. I have on my desk a copy of one of the best-known works of the Language movement. It's entitled *My Life* and the front cover is entirely taken up by the author's photograph!

In the real world there's a card-carrying self that's singular and stable enough to incur political responsibilities, that suffers injustice, or speaks out against it. Like other counterintuitive truisms of fundamentalist postmodernism – that writing precedes speech, or that there is no perception unmediated by language – the disappearance of the authorial subject has a perverse appeal for the faithful. It's the appeal of the oxymoron, or more exactly of Tertullian's rule of faith – *Certum est, quia impossibile* – it's certain because it's impossible, it's nonsense so it must be true.

The 'I' of my work may be equivocal, but the work remains speech based, gesture based, presence based. As I see it, the current fundamentalist pomo position proceeds from Derrida's rejection of Husserl's interpretation of Being-as-presence based on the proximity of voice to the body. Instead, Derrida famously asserts the counterprivilege of writing over Husserl's ontology of presence and acquisitive self-presence. But my commitment to voice and presence, and my particular take on oral traditions, heteronymity, the mask or visage, and the 'I' of the poem, are perhaps better understood with reference to Emmanuel Levinas. For Levinas, the primordial act is the recognition of the other, and the 'I' is not validated by the proximity of a voice to its own body, but by perceiving the voice of the 'Other' – all of which will eventually bring us back to the *Phaedrus* and issues of writing and speech. But perhaps we're getting a little far afield here. All this talk of philosophy suggests I have a programme. I don't. My poems are not illustrations. There's no agenda prior to what I work out through my negotiation with the verse.

You had a working life in the States as a doorman, which you refer to in your poem 'Local 32B'. What effect does that have on your work/outlook?

Well, the poem you refer to is just a joke, and that was only one of altogether too many jobs I've held. I've worked in factories and libraries, I've been a janitor, a musician, and yes, between 1972 and 1977 I wore a ridiculous uniform and worked as a doorman at a residential building on Fifth Avenue in Manhattan. Reading on the job was forbidden, but during the summer we were allowed to hold rather than wear our hats, so I kept a book hidden inside the crown. One day I placed my hat on a bench as a resident was entering and she noticed I was reading Hopkins. She turned out to be the treasurer of the famous poetry reading series at the 92nd St. 'Y' and she gave me a subscription to the Poetry Centre as a gift. I'd never been to a reading before, but within a month I'd seen Borges and Bunting. I suppose this was my conversion.

In my own case my early reading seems to me to have been about a different thing than my reading now. Miroslav Holub once asked me if I wrote for consolation. Well, I certainly started reading poetry for that. I wonder what it was first drew you to poetry.

Intoxication. My earliest influences were either intoxicatingly strange twentieth-century poets – Dylan Thomas, Wallace Stevens – or sixteenth- and seventeenth-century poets I read for the heady mysteries of their language. I'm not sure I've ever outgrown that initial attraction, though my tastes have changed somewhat. I'm equally fascinated by the poetry implicit in everyday speech and I'm just as likely to be bored spitless by 'difficulty' nowadays, particularly the current variety of emotionally anaemic pomo noodling that comes bundled with its own academic-career prose. I'm still most attracted to work of 'the first intensity', to the astonishing. What moves me to write now? Love, grief, curiosity – the usual suspects.

You were brought up a Roman Catholic and this finds expression in your work, e.g. 'Reprimands' where the you of the poem is accused of shallow doubt. Is that a true reflection of your own beliefs? It sounds as if in common with many Catholics you find it hard not to be influenced by it even now. There's an earlier poem, 'Pentecost', that has that same metaphysical resonance, the conflation of the erotic and sacred in a tightly rhetorical structure: 'Though we command the language of desire, / The voice of ecstasy is not our own.' I read this as proceeding from a genuine religious impulse, not as a pastiche.

Well, earlier in this interview I mentioned the emotional intensity of my childhood experience of Catholicism and my later intellectual involvement with Neo-Thomism through the work of David Jones. But my interest in the transcendent as it appears in my work is not tied to Catholicism or indeed any culturally determined notion of divinity. It comes from direct experience.

Here's where I jeopardize my driving licence: I used to suffer what Arthur Deikman calls 'untrained-sensate' episodes – spontaneous exultation accompanied by intense synaesthesia. Apparently, it's not that unusual. It's just an accident of brain chemistry and it may be genetic – my father had them too. As I've aged these episodes have become far less frequent, but they've been the most significant experiences of my life. You could call these 'spiritual' experiences, though it's not an issue of religion, with its root in *ligare*, binding, but a recurring experience of ecstasy, *ex-stasis*, release. And these experiences always struck me as 'beyond language'.

In order to square my experience with my scepticism (and indeed, with the basic message of the literary theory I was absorbing) I researched the subject and found the medical literature a little thin on the ground. The problem, of course, is that this phenomenon is almost always described with an organized religious idiom or classified as schizophrenia and at this stage of my life I considered myself neither Catholic nor especially mad. Then I encountered the work of academic medical researchers like Deikman, Gill and Brennan, who devoted themselves to the experimental research of this phenomenon, analysing it on a theoretical and experimental level. A keyword in the theory is 'de-automatization', a concept Gill and Brennan developed from Hartman's analysis of the automatization of motor behaviour. This might remind you of the literary notion of 'defamiliarization' in Russian Formalist criticism, but it's really quite different.

Hartman showed that efficient organisms 'automate' the somatic systems involved in motor activity and that with repeated exercise of the act they eliminate the intermediate steps from their consciousness. To quote Gill and Brennan, 'de-automatization is an undoing of the automatizations of apparatuses – both means and goal structures – directed toward the environment'. And this applies not only to motor behaviour but also to perception and thinking.

Deikman distinguishes between two modes of consciousness, the active and receptive (not to be confused with active vs passive or with the secondary and primary processes of psychoanalytic theory). When you drive, for example, you're in the active mode. You narrow your attention to the road. Your base-line muscle tension is high and your EEG records a desynchronized pattern. But in the receptive mode, your use of attention for abstract categorization is suppressed and reinvested in perception. Your consciousness features a marked decrease in the distinction between self and environment, you experience a nonverbal perception of unity, your

EEG will record alpha and theta waves, and most significantly, the mechanism of language is relinquished. Dante famously describes such an experience in the *Paradiso* when he sees Beatrice and is momentarily lifted from the realm of language: '*Trasumanar significar per verba / non si poria*' – the 'transhuman' state of grace may not be reduced to words.

Most religious mystics or survivors of schizophrenic episodes say that the experience is 'beyond words'. In fact, their experience is anterior to language. As a species we dominate because of our forebrain, our consciousness, at the expense of instinct. For all Chomsky says of our innate linguistic ability, the fact is we're born inarticulate but with an enormously open and receptive consciousness, which makes our offspring terribly vulnerable for longer than any other primate's. The language we rapidly learn is a survival mechanism and a powerful evolutionary advantage, like an opposable thumb. We learn to name and demand food, for example, and we use language to discriminate, to analyse, and to divide the world into objects that we can grasp and use. The variety or paucity of our vocabulary for any particular experience reflects these active or receptive modes. In English, for example, we have an enormous vocabulary for trade and finance, but only one word for love, despite its infinite variety, because love is experienced only in the receptive mode.

As Guillen said, '*Nombres estan sobre la patina de las cosas*' – names are a patina, a film, on the surface of things. But I believe there are particular uses of language that disrupt the patina, that momentarily short-circuit automatization and afford glimpses of that lost infantile consciousness, an experience that can be ecstatic or nightmarish. And this, I believe, is one of the functions of verse, and it may even be that verse has an evolutionary purpose. Many of the mnemonic features of verse push us into processing words in a receptive way. For example, the other day I came across this sentence in a textbook on genetics: 'The seeds of the individual fruit are easily calculated but it's impossible to estimate the number of mature fruit that will result from the germination of any one seed.' This may seem like an economical parcel of information, but to phrase it in a memorizable way we need something more like: 'We can count the seeds inside the apple, but who can count the apples in the seed?' The second formulation might be a handy mnemonic for the revising botany student, but it also carries a resonance beyond its denotative botanical meaning. Of course, it's now a soundbite, and I can imagine it used as advertising copy for Apple computers, or another inspirational platitude of some New Age guru – in fact, I believe a more devout version of this slogan is attributed to a US TV evangelist. But the fact is it does branch out toward a number of philosophical and spiritual meanings. In other words, by focusing more sharply on the image (apple rather than fruit) and by rephrasing the information in powerfully resonant patterns (chiasmus, iambic pentameter) we enlist the receptive mode.

You've spoken elsewhere of the political implications of this resonance. Reading poems like 'Ramon Fernandez?', 'Auto Da Fe' or 'Reliquary' I get a sense this is an abiding theme. I mean, you're suspicious of poetry's subliminal effects, no?

Yes. The example I gave above could also just as easily be dropped into a keynote speech at a party conference. You may recall that at Kennedy's inauguration Frost read 'The Gift Outright' which began with the lines 'The land was ours before we were the land's . . . Possessing what we still were unpossessed by, / Possessed by what we now no more possessed'. Minutes afterwards, the president who was to send Americans into Vietnam stood on the same platform and urged them to stop asking questions and serve the State: 'Ask not what your country can do for you. Ask what you can do for your country.' So Kennedy found the chiasmus or antimetabole Frost used in the service of truth a handy tool for political propaganda. That is, for as long as it took to say it, Kennedy's speech had all the symmetry and closure of logic.

All the techniques of verse – metre, rhyme, rhetorical tropes and schemes – evolved as mnemonic techniques to aid the poet or orator in both composition and memorization for oral delivery. But they also help fix poets' words in the minds of the audience. And this operation occurs below the level of reason. Here's the question: if rational political discourse is best served by prose and if the most powerful techniques of poetry are tricks of subliminal persuasion, how do we justify poetry as a political instrument? How can the 'receptive state' challenge the State? I've got some ideas, but I'd prefer to address that issue through my poems rather than spell it all out here.

You've said in Poetry Review *that your poems are about 'music, sex and drinking', which makes you sound like Charles Bukowski. Why did you choose to describe – I would say misrepresent – your work that way?*

I have an early poem called 'Music Sex and Drinking' in which these are metaphors for, among other things, the pursuit of ecstasy. Alcohol is a common enough metaphor for spiritual exultation. Think of Dickinson's 'liquor never brewed' or the 'divine intoxication of the first league out from land'. Or think of St John of the Cross, who describes his soul as 'the interior wine cellar of my Beloved'. Pope lampoons the poetic diction of 'Set Bacchus from his glassy prison free' but we can trace that image back through history to Dionysus, who was also called Theoinus, 'god-wine' – the wine itself, in other words, was the god. And yes, before you ask, I take a drink now and then.

And what though has this notion of the ecstatic to do with poetry? Is the person described in Keats's 'Ode on Melancholy' the true poet, he who can experience the agony and the ecstasy, so to speak? Or the visionary of whom we are advised to weave a circle thrice round by another romantic poet? Is this part of the impulse of the poetic sensibility? Is there such a thing?

No. We haven't even got as far as defining poetry, so we'd be pretty foolish to expound on the 'poetic sensibility'. But since you mention Keats, melancholy, and ecstasy in one breath, I'll admit to an interest in this. I think the 'Ode on Melancholy' is one of the most remarkable poems in the language for its psychological subtlety. In warning his auditor not to hunt for the goddess Melancholy in the isles of Lethe, or seek her in drugged sleep, Keats is drawing a distinction between what we now call depression, a condition which drains significance from the world, and Melancholy, a wild passionate sadness which he describes in terms of fertility. There's a precedent for this in Milton, who sees 'divinist Melancholy / Whose saintly visage is too bright / To hit the sense of human sight' whom he asks to 'Dissolve [him] into ecstasies'. All of which reminds me of the Japanese notion of *mono no aware*, that exquisite sadness induced by the sight of clouds passing in the sky, by the cherry blossom that blooms for three days before scattering. The Heian master Kukai taught that only such fragile mortal beauty can reveal the Buddha's truth: all that lives must suffer and die.

Yes, I notice a lot of Japanese references in your work – the ritual suicide of a tea master, an incense contest, etc. Is Japanese Buddhism an influence?

It is. But you can work that out from my previous answers. I'm also simply drawn to the aesthetic, to the delicacy, the minimalism, the tension of the compositional asymmetry. I studied Japanese art for a term as an undergraduate and spent some time studying *byobu* – painted folding screens – of the Muromachi and Momoyama periods. I was also very taken with Pound's translations of Noh plays and Yeats's Noh-influenced 'moon mysteries'.

You're most often described as a 'modern metaphysical'. It seems to me this is a description you invite, comparing a baroque pavanne to a bicycle or quoting Marvell's 'On A Drop of Dew', for example, in 'Our Life Stories' . . . 'This marvellous drop, like its own tear' . . .

He's generally regarded as more secular than Herbert, and certainly not as a visionary like Traherne or Vaughan, but I find the way Marvell gestures toward the ineffable tremendously ingenious and compelling, perhaps because of his very worldliness. 'The Garden', for example, is a serious poem about religious experience, but he sees no reason to articulate the experience solemnly. He performs his devotion wittily, the same way Donne constructs a serious love poem around what amounts to an ingenious joke, and for both poets I find this strategy intensifies, rather than diminishes, the emotional power of the poems.

Look at the way 'The Garden' unfolds. The speaker retires into the cool shade of the garden, withdrawing his attention from the heat and dust of the world and he passes into what I described earlier as a receptive state; 'What wond'rous Life in this I lead! / Ripe Apples drop about my head; / The Luscious Clusters of the Vine / Upon My Mouth do crush their Wine'. Free of the 'uncessant Labours' of the active realm of power and desire, he finds apples drop from the trees and grapes crush themselves on his mouth, an image that may have crossed Keats's mind when he was composing the 'Ode On Melancholy' – prelapsarian innocence is momentarily restored, and he progresses to a direct contemplation of God 'Annihilating all that's made / To a green Thought in a green Shade'.

As for courting the designation 'metaphysical', yes, guilty as charged. Twentieth-century academics, from Cleanth Brooks to Geoffrey Hartman, have embraced the highly teachable metaphysical lyric, and all this interest began with that covert manifesto, Eliot's 1921 review of Grierson's anthology. So the voice performing the syllogistic gestures of 'Pentecost' or 'Machines' appears to be calling us back to that crossroads in taste, laying claim to a certain authority and demanding our attention and critical scrutiny. But of course, that rather preening voice is only one of many you might hear, and I hope it's balanced by the others.

The past falls open anywhere. 'Black Ice and Rain' is a dramatic monologue which tells the story of a kind of three-way relationship and its fate. How fictional can that sort of story be and what is the relation in your work between the historically true, the personal/private, the confessional and the purely fictional? A recent poem 'From The Safe House' has a different kind of relation to the past, i.e. it is made clear in the poem itself that the primary account is fictional and that things didn't happen that way. But did they happen the other way either?

This is the most difficult question to answer. As I've said elsewhere, I'm bound by the sanctity of the confessional – not as in 'confessional poetry' but the box where the sacrament is conducted. I know that quoting Wittgenstein or making analogies with quantum physics is the last refuge of a charlatan, but I have to say that I want my work to exist in a state of quantum uncertainty. Schrödinger's cat is behind the curtain of that confessional box.

Yes, the second and third lines of your most recent book are 'My father's sudden death has shocked us all / Even me, and I've just made it up'. Yet these poems still move me.

Good. If these poems work, they're 'about' the reader, not about me. All poets gather details from life, of course, but only confessional poets are *defined* by their simulation of sincerity. Lowell, for example, admitted in a *Paris Review* interview that he 'tinkered' with the facts in *Life Studies* but that 'the reader was to believe he was getting the real Robert Lowell'. In the lines you quote I'm warning the reader not to expect 'the real Michael Donaghy' in any documentary sense. I'm not sure I'm a reliable narrator of events even to myself. Just as poets' ideal readers are always ghostly composites of themselves, their contemporaries, deceased influences, their friends and family, so readers must realize that poets, too, are ghostly compounds of fact and invention. So a story I write from the point of view of a Japanese courtesan or an early Christian saint may be as or more autobiographical than a poem about the death of my father.

Your poem 'Palm' involves an imagined scenario in which Paul de Man is cuckolded by Django Reinhardt. The imaginary meeting, or almost meeting, in that poem is characteristic of strategies that go by the name of postmodernism in contemporary poetry. Is this a term you recognize in relation to your own work? How does this fit with formalism and respect for tradition? I've read that you were once turned out of a lecture by de Man.

While the phrase 'respect for tradition' has great resonance for me as regards the music I love, it means nothing for me in regard to poetry. Does falling down indicate a respect for the law of gravity? Tradition is simply there whether I choose to respect it or not. In oral traditions in a community or national sense you conduct yourself in a manner akin to filial piety. I 'respect' such traditions because they're fragile and require respect. But the literary tradition we've inherited, though permeated by values of orality, is based on print. Literary resonance is a powerful tool for a poet, not an obligation. By the way, I never studied with de Man. The incident you mention was trivial and unrelated to literature. And as for 'postmodern', I believe that term is under copyright. I wouldn't presume to appropriate it.

But surely your work inhabits a postmodern space. That is to say where, with knowing artifice, the text draws attention to its own status as text, this manoeuvre being central to the conceit of the piece.

No, I mean it. 'Postmodernism' first appears as an architectural term as far back as the forties. In eighties architecture 'postmodern' meant radically eclectic – classical allusions, ornaments, etc. (I think my computer spell check has the right idea here when it changes postmodern to 'post-mortem'.) But if literary postmodernism merely means foregrounding artifice, the gap between signifier and signified, look at how long it's been around – Sterne, Swift, Coleridge, etc. . . . . Now the term's been used so consistently by a particular theory-led faction that I feel they're welcome to it. I'd be happier if you called me a 'paramodernist' – now there's a nice long word. The distinguishing characteristic of paramodernism, which I've just discovered this minute, is a suspicion of metanarrative, particularly that neat linear progression classical<romantic<modern<postmodern. I hereby decree that paramodernism involves exiting the funhouse of spatial

illusions, or at least acknowledging that you're in that funhouse, surrounded by distorting mirrors.

You've tried your hand at other art forms like film. Are you a paramodernist filmmaker as well?

Funding bodies are very interested in 'collaborations' nowadays, aren't they? I made a poem/film with Miranda Pennell, *Habit*, with the actress Fiona Shaw speaking my poem. I also played for a time in the jazz band Lammas with Don Paterson and I've worked with the *musique concrète* composer John Wall on a poem for voices using sampling techniques. I haven't got any immediate plans for further collaborations but I'd consider any offers.

You run a highly respected writing group in London from which a number of your students have gone on to publication and acclaim. But can you really teach the writing of poetry? Does the high volume of poetry you have to read in that case interfere with your own writing?

Yes to both questions. Of *course* poetry workshops are useful. No one doubts that music can be taught because there's so much quantifiable technique imparted at the conservatory. An apprenticeship in poetry requires a more oblique process, but there are so many ways a mentor can help. Naturally, you can't make people rigorous, sensitive or witty. But you can finesse them out of cul de sacs or suggest poems they might want to read or train them in habits of reading. I'm lucky in that I'm completely free in my workshops – I can devote an entire evening to the examination of a particular poem or critical perspective, or to the study of the evolution of a particular trope through history, and no department head calls me in to tell me I have to devote more time to *The Maximus Poems*. Of course, we spend the balance of every workshop on discussions of student work. And yes, the attention I give to student work might be more profitably spent on my own poetry. But it's still the best job I've ever had.

Last question. You perform your work from memory, a lot of your poems are built around physical gestures, and I notice you're not above playing the odd bit of music during your performances. Are you a performance poet?

Maybe I am. It all began a few years ago when I turned up for a reading having left my books on the train – at which point I realized to my mild horror that I'd inadvertently memorized my poems – I suppose this is because I'd taken such a long time composing them. So I just stood there and said them. I recall being inordinately worried how this would appear to the audience. Would I come across as conceited, theatrical, unliterary? Back then I had a puritanical prejudice against recitation. Reading from a text, preferably from behind a mahogany lectern, seemed more scholarly, more serious, more dignified. I felt there was something intrinsically narcissistic and hammy about performance. But when I began to speak I realized I was completing the action that began with my decision to write in a memorizable form. The words fell into place – catch that spatial analogy – and I realized there was another level to this art.

When I say 'puritanical prejudice', by the way, I'm being fastidious. The reformation and the rise of print led directly to the denigration of older oral, performative methods of communication, to the suppression of theatre, and the campaign against 'enthusiasm' in preaching, against gesture and spoken rhetoric. It remains a deep-seated bias of the bookish or literary personality. I went on tour last year with the queen of dub poetry, Jean 'Binta' Breeze, and I was struck by her unabashed use of movement and song. She reminded me of Pindar's description of Greek poetry performance as sacred debt: 'to blend together properly the lyre with her intricate voice, and the shout of oboes, and the placing of words.' By contrast, I'm fairly monochrome in my performance, but I now acknowledge that the art I practise is related to μουσιχη, *mousiké*, 'the art of the Muses', a term which referred equally to music, words and dance. But the term 'performance poet' makes my heart sink. A bad performance poet is the worst kind of nuisance, and a dynamic performer can make the worst doggerel sound profound to an aurally naive audience. Nevertheless, I ought to face the fact that when I stand before an audience, I'm a performer. I know I should accept the designation gracefully, but it still rankles. That's showbiz.

Acknowledgements

Acknowledgement is gratefully made to the editors of the following periodicals and publications, in which pieces have appeared:

CRITICISM AND REVIEWS

'The Liberal Line' – *Poetry Review* vol 79/1
'Rhyme Crime USA' – *Poetry Review* vol 81/4
'Crashing the Devil's Party' – *Poetry Review* vol 87/2
'Criticism and Hedonism' – *Poetry Review* vol 83/2
'The Exile's Accent' – *Elizabeth Bishop: Poet of the Periphery* edited
    by Linda Anderson and Jo Shapcott, Bloodaxe (2002)

MISCELLANEOUS PIECES

'My Report Card' in *Strong Words: Modern Poets on Modern Poetry*
    edited by W. N. Herbert and Matthew Hollis, Bloodaxe (2000)
'A Backward Glance' in *Poetry Review* vol 79/3
'All Poets Are Mad' in *Mortification: Writers' Stories of Their Public
    Shame* edited by Robin Robertson, Fourth Estate (2003)
'Introduction' to *The May Anthologies: Poetry: 2001* edited by
    Michael Donaghy, Varsity Publications (2001)
'Introduction' to *101 Poems About Childhood* edited by Michael
    Donaghy, Faber and Faber (2005)
'May I Make a Suggestion?' in *Poetry London Newsletter*, Autumn
    1998
'The Questionnaire' in *Poetry Review* vol 92/4

Acknowledgements

INTERVIEWS

Interview with John Wall in *Verse* vol 14/1 1997
Interview with Conor O'Callaghan in *Metre* no 4 1997
Interview with Andy Brown in *Binary Myths: Conversations with
    Contemporary Poets* edited by Andy Brown, Stride Publications
    (1998)
Interview with Nick Cobic in *The Wolf*, issue 1 2002